J   Burton, Hester.
Beyond the weir bridge. Illustrated by Victor G. Ambrus. New York, Crowell [1970, ©1969]

x, 221 p. illus. 24 cm. 4.50

Three young people in seventeenth-century England maintain their
close friendship despite their political and religious differences, the
tragedy of the Great Plague, and the two boys' rivalry for the girl's
love.

1. Gt. Brit.—History—Stuarts, 1603-1714 - Fiction
Gt.—History—Stuarts, 1603-1714—Fiction,   i. Ambrus, Victor G.,
illus.   I. Title.

PZ7.B953Be 3   [Fic]   WH5/71   77-109906
ISBN 0-690-14052-5   MARC

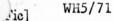

Beyond the
❋ Weir Bridge

Thomas Y. Crowell Company ❀ *New York*

Beyond the
Weir Bridge

J

cl

By Hester Burton

illustrated by Victor G. Ambrus

❀

First published in the United States of
America in 1970
Originally published in Great Britain
under the title *Thomas*

Copyright © 1969 by *Hester Burton*

Designed by Carole Fern Halpert

Manufactured in the United States of
America

L.C. Card 77-109906
ISBN 0-690-14052-5

1   2   3   4   5   6   7   8   9   10

For Mabel George

❋ Author's Note

All the characters in this story are fictional except for Margaret, widow of Judge Fell of Swarthmoor Hall, who later married George Fox, the famous Quaker.

The background, however, against which these characters move—and the trials which they had to endure—are as historically accurate as I, living three centuries later, am able to make them. Luckily, the years 1651–67, covered by the story, are exceptionally rich in diaries, journals, and autobiographies. In trying to recreate the period, I have learned much from the writings of Anthony à Wood, John Aubrey, John Evelyn, Samuel Pepys, and the Verney family. For details of domestic life, I am indebted to E. Godfrey's *Home Life Under the Stuarts*, and for particulars about the seventeenth-century grammar schools, I am indebted to Foster Watson's paper *The English Grammar Schools to 1660, Their Curriculum and Practice*.

The sufferings of the Quakers of this period are particularly well documented. Among the most rewarding sources, I found the contemporary account given in George Fox's *Journal* and Thomas Ellwood's *Life*. I am indebted, also, to two works of modern scholarship: Isabel Ross's *Margaret Fell, Mother of Quakerism* (Longmans, Green, 1949) and William Braithwaite's exhaustive *The Second Period of Quakerism* (*1660–1714*) (Macmillan, 1921).

My information about the plague of London comes from Walter Bell's *The Great Plague of London, 1665* (John Lane and Bodley Head, 1924).

❖ Note on the English Civil War

Some readers may not be familiar with the historical events which form the background of this story. The English Civil War (1642–1651) was the outcome of a long-standing quarrel between the Crown and Parliament over the extent to which Parliament should share in the government of the country. When Parliament, in 1641, demanded wide constitutional changes and the raising of an army controlled by Parliament and not by the king, King Charles I refused to agree and, in the following year, gathered a small army of his own to challenge Parliament's power. Civil warfare broke out.

The king's men were called Royalists or Cavaliers; his opponents Roundheads (because they cut their hair short), Puritans, or Parliament Men. Most of King Charles's support came from great landowners and their tenants, including the Roman Catholic minority, in the North and West of the country. The greatest strength of Parliament was in the East and South, among merchants, smaller landowners, and yeoman farmers, many of whom were Puritan in religion. But there was no exact geographical or social division.

After Charles I's final defeat and execution on January 30, 1649, his son, Charles II, carried on the war with the help of his Scottish allies. But after their disastrous defeat at the Battle of Worcester on September 3, 1651, the young king fled to France and the Civil War came to an end. Oliver Cromwell, the great Parliament military commander, ruled supreme.

The story of *Beyond the Weir Bridge* opens six days after the Battle of Worcester, while the fugitive young king was still making his way in disguise to the south coast of England.

Adapted from *The Oxford Junior Encyclopaedia*

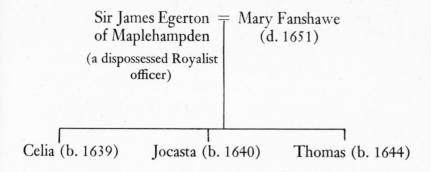

Sir James Egerton = Mary Fanshawe
of Maplehampden   (d. 1651)
(a dispossessed Royalist
officer)

Celia (b. 1639)   Jocasta (b. 1640)   Thomas (b. 1644)

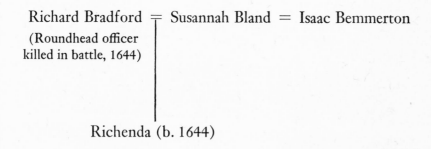

Richard Bradford = Susannah Bland = Isaac Bemmerton
(Roundhead officer
killed in battle, 1644)

Richenda (b. 1644)

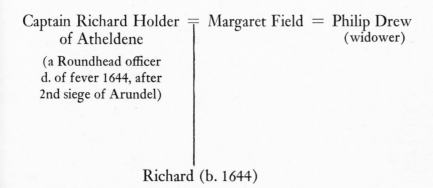

Captain Richard Holder = Margaret Field = Philip Drew
of Atheldene   (widower)
(a Roundhead officer
d. of fever 1644, after
2nd siege of Arundel)

Richard (b. 1644)

❉ Contents

Beyond the
❁ Weir Bridge

1
❀ Maplehampden

RICHARD Holder never forgot his first coming to Maplehampden. Every detail of the visit remained sharp in his mind. The great house. The river. The upward curve of the beech-covered Chiltern Hills. Even the quaint little net cap that Richenda was wearing. All were imprisoned in radiance, like flies caught in amber.

The distinctness of his memory puzzled him in after years, for there had been so many other things that he might have remembered from his childhood. Hateful, unspeakable things.

Richard had been born in the blackened ruin of his father's house at Atheldene, a bare week after his father's death in battle. And, if this were but a hearsay grief told him by Marty, his nurse, it was not so with the other horrors of the times. He and his mother and Marty had spent the next five years journeying fitfully through an England torn by civil war. The blare of trumpets, the distant booming of guns, and the smell of smoldering farms were part and parcel of his early life. When he was four years old he had heard the clatter of horses' hoofs in the lane below his grandmother's house. Marty had clutched him in her arms, and together they had listened to the soldiers dismounting and shouting to one another as they surrounded his grandmother's barn. They had clung to each other in an agony of fear, knowing that the troopers had come to shoot the two wounded deserters who had crept into the hayloft earlier that day. A volley of musket-fire. The scream of women. The tears running down old Marty's face. What more was there to learn of the bitterness of war?

Yet there *was* more—much more.

Three months later, in a summer season, he was running through a sea of grass. The sun was hot on his head. There was a buzzing of bees. He was laughing. He was making for the buttercups which grew along the ditch. On its very brink he had stumbled and fallen on his knees. And there he had remained, staring and staring, struck with wonder and alarm at the white-faced bundle of uniform, moldering and forgotten in the ditch. He had not understood at first what it was that he saw. And then he knew. It was death. It was what happened to men when they were dead.

Next morning his mother had hurried them away, first to Norwich, then to Bedford, then to London—where they had often been before. And it was in London, on a bitter January day just before he was five, that she had come to him as he sat on an oriental rug in a dark-panelled room, tracing the letters on his hornbook—her voice high and her eyes bright with triumph.

"They have cut off the arch-tyrant's head!" she exclaimed.

"Who's the arch-tyrant?" he had asked absently, finishing the rich bulge of the letter "O."

"The king, you fool," she had rasped, tapping him sharply over his head with her bunch of keys.

She was always maddened by his childishness.

"Your father's enemy, the *king,* you dolt," she had shouted, turning from him in exasperation.

King Charles I's death had meant nothing at all to him. If the king had been his father's foe, then it was right that men should cut off his head. It was as simple as that.

But he had winced at the pain of the bunch of keys—and at his mother's lack of love.

Yet it was Maplehampden—not the war, nor his mother—which was caught in that shaft of light.

Perhaps it was small wonder, after all. For it was at Maplehampden, down by the River Thames, on that autumn day in 1651, that Thomas and Richenda first burst into his life.

It was then that the three of them made their wordless pact.

Then that their strange story began.

The young Charles II had been defeated at the Battle of Worcester six days before and on that same afternoon was slipping, disguised, from one safe hiding-place to the next on his way to the coast. General Cromwell's soldiers were out scouring the countryside for the fugitive king. As the coach plunged over the open stubble field and rounded the bend in the river, old Mr. Bemmerton pointed out a troop of them caught on the skyline on the ridge of Hampden Hill.

"We ought never to have come!" Richard's mother had exclaimed. "Never! Not at a time like this!"

The Egertons were Royalists. The accursed Charles Stuart, she said, might even now be lying hid in Maplehampden House. They might all of them be suspected. Disgraced. Undone.

Mr. Bemmerton shook his head and drove on.

"The wars are over," he replied gently. "And they need us now."

Snap, snap, went the dry stubble under the carriage wheels. Above them, the silent beech trees seemed to hang upon the hills. Richenda, sitting opposite him, swung her slippered feet to the lurching of the clumsy coach and scowled her swift, strange scowl.

"Mary Egerton was our friend, Margaret," her mother said. "Our childhood friend."

"Childhood's a long time ago!" Richard's mother burst out bitterly.

He felt ashamed of her, he remembered. His cheeks ablaze, he stared down over the wheels of the coach at the scarlet pimpernels clustered round the bottom of the wheat stalks. They were growing pale in the bleaching sun. He wondered angrily why his father had not given him a mother of whom he could be proud. A strong, quiet mother, like Richenda's.

But it was not his mother's selfish fears nor yet the soldiers hunting the young king that set that day apart. It was not the grown-ups' world that he saw in his memory. It was their own: the children's. It was Richenda and Thomas and himself—all aged seven—who reached out their hands to him across the years.

This was how it was.

Over the weir, not three feet above the water, stretched a narrow plank bridge, less than a foot wide. It was used by the watermen when they cleared the reeds and dead leaves brought down by the winter gales.

Richard took one look at the roaring fall of water and the rickety thing that spanned it and felt the challenge of them both. Yet, to speak truth, it was more than a challenge. And worse. For he had stared in amazement at Thomas at their first meeting, and then stared at his father's great house, and had been stabbed by the injustice of so puny a boy—a Royalist at that—being heir to so much, while he—Richard Holder—had nothing at all.

That mad crossing of the weir was done to shame Thomas.

"I wager you've never done this," he hurled back at him, as he ran out over the River Thames.

The distance between one stout post driven into the river-bed and the next was so wide that the single plank that spanned the gap bent down and swung up under the weight of his running, as though it were alive. It surprised him. It took away his breath. On his right the river slid towards him, smooth and smiling and full of guile. On his left it roared downwards six feet or more into an angry whirl of white waters. He must hurry, hurry, he thought in a sudden flurry of fear, or else the plank would bounce him off into the water. His ears buzzed. It came to him that he had been a fool. A great fool. He vowed that he would never do such a stupid thing again. Never. Out in the middle of the river the roar of the weir seemed to batter all sense out of his head. The falling water was tugging at him to follow it down into the tumbling race below. In a last excess of fear, he made a wild lunge for the Berkshire bank. And the rickety bridge, as if in sport, tossed him up and forward through the air into a bank of Berkshire nettles.

He was so relieved to be alive that he scarcely noticed their prickling. He felt drunk with triumph.

"Thomas!" he shouted exultantly, jumping up and pushing the hair out of his eyes.

Thomas was already a third of the way out across the river, looking white in the face. He was putting one foot down very carefully in front of the other and spreading out his arms like a tightrope-walker he had once seen at a country fair.

How strange is one's mind! As he watched that puny, frightened figure poised above the flashing river, Richard's anger and contempt were gone. He felt only a horrible fear that Thomas was going to lose his balance and be drowned. He was half-way out now from the Oxfordshire bank. The roar of the weir must be battering his brain. The falling water must be tugging at those slow, deliberate feet. He felt sick with remorse. He could not bear to watch; and he could not bear to turn away. Suddenly, while he stared at him, the boy looked green all over; green, wavy blobs were dancing over his face and arms. Then, as he came nearer, Richard could see that Thomas was biting his lip. His dark hair was black with sweat.

He felt a desperate need to save Thomas from his fear. He leaned out from the bank and held out his hand.

"You did it much better than me," he laughed, trying to cover the boy's panic. "I was stupid to run.'"

Thomas gripped his hand, smiling faintly, his face still tense. Then, when he was safely on the bank—and he was assured that he as safe—he suddenly began chattering as fast as a magpie.

"I didn't know I could! I never did! And we went across. Right across. The very first time!"

Richard stared at him in astonishment. Thomas's brown eyes were flashing with pride.

"And Celia and Jocasta," he gabbled on. "They've *never* been across. And they're years older than me."

And with this, Thomas gave him a smile that he never forgot. It seemed strangely grateful and innocent, even then. No one had ever smiled like that at him before. Not even old Marty. It was a new sensation. It made him feel proud to be himself.

Both of them had forgotten Richenda.

Indeed, up to that moment—to tell the truth—Richard had scarcely ever remembered her. He had known her most of his life. Yet she had been a presence to him, rather than a person. A pleasurable presence—like sunlight. He had taken Richenda for granted.

And now, suddenly, there she was! Richenda herself! A girl in a net cap and a plain brown dress, far out above the river on that dangerous, rickety plank.

"Richenda!" shouted Thomas.

"Richenda! Go back. It's not safe," Richard yelled over the roaring weir.

Richenda might have been deaf. She walked on steadily in a sedate sort of dream, looking neither to right nor to left.

"We ought never to've done it," sobbed Thomas in despair. "We never ought."

It was Richard's fault. He knew it. As he watched her sleep-walking over the tumbling water, he felt a terrible ache. At the very moment of seeing her for the first time as herself, he realized what he had done to her. If Richenda fell off the plank and was drowned, he would have killed her. It was as terrible as that.

"Richenda!" shrieked Thomas, pointing frantically upstream. "Stand still. Don't move. There's a wind coming."

Richard could see what he meant. In the reach of the river under Hampden Hill the surface of the water was gray and puckered with the wind. The tops of the willows were bending before it. Richenda's long skirts would fill with the wind—like a sail.

She must have heard their shouts, yet she walked on over the bending plank bridge, her head held high and her blue eyes

mocking them both as they stood in panic on the Berkshire bank. Just as the wind reached her, she came to one of the stout posts driven into the river-bed. Here, on this firmer planking, she stopped, stooped down, and held the skirts of her dress close round her legs, and waited for the valley wind to pass.

She came to them as calmly as though she had been walking in the lime avenue at Benfield.

Thomas flung his arms round her and burst into tears.

"Girls aren't stupider than boys," she said haughtily. "Did you think I'd be silly and fall off?"

Richard remembered that, with the terror now behind him, he had felt mortified by Thomas's embrace. He had never dreamed of throwing his arms round Richenda's neck. He felt cheated, somehow, and left behind. And later, when they were walking in the Berkshire marsh and Richenda had run ahead of them to gather the last of the marsh flowers, he had burst out angrily to his new friend:

"I've known Richenda far longer than you have. I've known her ever since we were born."

Thomas had looked up at him, both puzzled and hurt.

"Why are you angry?" he had asked.

"Because you behave as if Richenda belongs to you," he had replied. "And she doesn't. She's mine as well."

Thomas had walked on, frowning. He had pulled at the dying heads of the meadow-sweet, letting the dry seeds fall through his fingers. Richard could see him now: a dark, sad boy, much smudged round the eyes with grief. He must still have been shocked by his mother's death.

"It's just that I want to protect her," Thomas said slowly. "I want to protect Richenda all my life."

Richard had looked at him in astonishment—and then smiled. For Thomas was so wizened and thin at the time that he could not have protected a pet mouse.

"You had better leave it to me to look after Richenda," he had replied grandly. "I'm bigger and stronger than you."

Richenda remembered that far-off autumn day as clearly as Richard, but because she was a girl she remembered quite different things.

She remembered the excitement of their setting out from Benfield. Not even Lady Egerton's death could damp the joy of going to Maplehampden once again.

"You will meet Thomas," she had whispered to Richard as they climbed into her stepfather's coach. "You will like Thomas. I know you will."

And then, as the old coach rumbled and shook over the stubble field, she had suddenly been assailed by a terrible fear.

Why should Richard like Thomas? What if he hated him, instead?

She looked at Richard sitting opposite her. He was square and strong. He was so strong, in fact, and so excited by his strength that he sometimes knocked one over by mistake. She had known him all her life, for he had come to her stepfather's house in London—and stayed very often for months on end. They had shared their first lessons; they had played together in the little walled court at the back. Yet, until this moment, she had never really thought what he was *like*. He was just Richard. Her friend.

Then she thought of Thomas. And she frowned.

The sun poured down on the wooded hills; the heat shimmered over the top of the stubble stalks. Her frown grew deeper and deeper. She was filled with panic. Swaying there in the coach, she suddenly realized that people were not just friends or relations or servants. They were themselves; they were different. They existed on their own. In a flash, she saw that Richard was quick and kind—but also, a clumsy braggart. He must always be first; he must always win. And Thomas? In the same quick light, she saw that Thomas never cared whether he came first or last. He was quite different from Richard.

"Look, my dears, just look!" her stepfather had exclaimed.

They had all followed his gaze to the hills. Richenda had seen the sunlight glint on the soldiers' helmets and pikes.

"It must be the troopers out looking for the young Charles Stuart."

She had long been bored by the grown-ups' wars. She gave hardly a thought to the plight of the fugitive king. She was obsessed by her doubts.

"What if Richard thinks Thomas is a milksop?" she asked herself wretchedly. "What if Thomas thinks Richard nothing but a bullying fool?"

Down by the river, her worst fears had been realized, for Richard had stood and stared at Thomas in ill-disguised contempt, while Richenda herself suddenly saw her new friend growing smaller and whiter in front of her eyes. She had felt angry with them both and furious with herself. And then, before she could guess what he was at, Richard had run far out over the plank bridge and was hurling back taunts at the grave and puzzled Thomas left standing by her side.

"He's a fool. Don't take any notice," she had muttered to Thomas. "He does it as a boast."

She might have been talking to the river gnats.

Thomas had already left her and was stepping gingerly onto the trembling plank in Richard's bouncing wake.

Richenda had never felt so frightened before. Thomas was clumsy with his feet. She knew he was clumsy. The Thames was full to flooding after last week's rain, and the water thundered over the weir. She would never forgive Richard. Never. As she watched Thomas's outstretched hands and fumbling steps, she felt a yawning ache in the pit of her stomach. She wanted to cry out in pain; in warning; in anger. Yet she knew she must not make a sound. Just wait and watch—and pray. Pray that he would not tumble off and drown.

Looking back on that memorable day, she realized that it had been full of surprises. For hardly had she sighed with relief at seeing Thomas safely past the weir and Richard's hand outstretched to help him ashore than she had felt herself swept by uncontrollable indignation. How dare they have given her such a fright! And how dare they have forgotten her! But it was worse than forgetting. The two boys had dismissed her as someone too weak and too timid to follow them over the river.

She bit her lip in anger and marched out boldly over the tumbling water.

She would teach them to despise a girl.

And then, when the terror was over and the weir roared safely behind them all, she had danced off into the marsh, intoxicated by joy.

All was well. Richard and Thomas were friends.

The myriad sounds and sights and smells of the marsh rose to greet her. The hum of bees and gnats and midges; the plop of frogs in the water, the flash of dragonfly wings, the heady smell of the ooze seemed to swell into a paean of praise as the glory of the day broke over her head. The sun had never shone so brightly. Maplehampden and its water meadows had never looked more beautiful. Richard and Thomas were friends. Everything was right. It had never been better to be alive.

Looking up from gathering the last of the willow-herb, she peered over the feathery tops of the reeds at the great house basking on the farther bank, rose-red and glowing in the warm autumnal light. The pointed gables over the two wings looked like ears, the wide oak door like a nose.

"Oh, look at your house, Thomas!" she shouted. "It looks like a cat."

The two boys caught up with her, and the three of them stood staring at the wonder of Maplehampden and the reflection of that wonder mirrored in the river, silent at first, awed by the beauty of the sight.

Then Richard blurted out:

"But the windows are all broken on the ground floor. Why doesn't your father have them mended?"

Richenda blushed for Richard's stupid question. She knew its answer. So did Thomas. But he was too proud to give it.

"How do we get back across the river?" she had asked hurriedly, to change the subject.

"I'm not going back over that rotten plank," declared Richard roundly. "No one would."

"But there isn't another bridge for miles, is there?" she asked Thomas.

Not one of them wanted to face again the terror that they had just left behind.

"There's the ford," Thomas had smiled quickly. "We can take off our shoes and stockings and wade. Follow me."

They had set off on the instant, walking in single file along the reed-cutters' path, Richenda sniffing in the rank smell of the river weed as she went.

"It's lovely. It's lovely," she had thought. "It smells fishy and full of eels."

Everything about the country delighted her after smoky London and its acrid smell of sea coal.

"Here it is," said Thomas, stopping at last. "This is where we cross."

Richenda remembered that she had gathered up her skirts contemptuously under her arms as they waded over the shingly bar.

They had crossed now to the back of the great house, and, as they walked up the long elm avenue, Richard's remark about the broken windows must have still rankled in Thomas's mind.

"That's where the Roundheads rode across," he announced with melancholy pride, jerking his head back in the direction of the ford. "And they fought a great battle under the house windows. Father and the tenants and Captain Longford . . ."

"Poor Thomas!" she had thought swiftly, suddenly comprehending the depth of his hurt pride. His father's friends had lost the war. Their king had lost his head. And now, Thomas's mother was dead. Everywhere there was defeat. And the sting and shame and poverty of defeat. There was not even the money to mend the window-panes. She looked across at Richard quickly, praying that he, too, understood how it was with Thomas and the Egertons.

But Richard had not understood. His face bore its scornful look. It could not have been a great battle that Sir James had fought here at Maplehampden, his face said plainly. Perhaps just a skirmish. Nothing more.

"And father drove them off," continued Thomas proudly. "He sent the Roundheads all galloping back to Reading with a gadfly in their tails."

Richard and Richenda caught each other's eye. Then, together, they turned and looked at Thomas.

There was no spite in Thomas. There never was. And because they saw there was no spite, the two of them—both made fatherless by the Royalists even before they were born—forebore to remind their friend of the fact.

"A gadfly, Thomas?" asked Richard, his face breaking into a wide and joyous smile. "Did you say a gadfly?"

Thomas lowered his eyes. He must have suddenly remembered how it was with them both.

"I think that's what father said," he mumbled, looking away embarrassed.

Richenda had wanted to throw her arms round him to give him comfort.

But she did nothing of the sort.

"Race you to the mill," she had shouted instead, turning on her heel and flashing barefoot round the wing of the house.

The wars were over. Her stepfather had said so. Besides, how could their fathers' wars ever be their own?

She remembered that the three of them had sat up in the dusty little loft above the broken mill wheel, breathless and crowded together and happy—linked in some kind of conspiracy against the rest of the world. They had heard the thudding of horses' hoofs on the cobbles in the mill yard. They had listened to the jingle of harness and the quick-spoken commands of the officer immediately below them.

"Sh!" Thomas had whispered, peeping through a crack in the shuttered window. "They've come to look for the king."

2
❖ Parents

ONE morning, six weeks later, when the autumn gales were blowing the leaves off the lime trees in the Benfield avenue and the skies lowered so darkly that Mr. Bemmerton had to sit in the parlor window for light to read his Greek Testament, the carrier's boy rode up from the village with a letter for Richenda's mother.

The address looked so crudely inscribed that Richenda was curious.

"Whom can it be from?" she asked as she handed it to her mother.

Mrs. Bemmerton broke the wax and took the letter to the window.

"It's from Marty!" she exclaimed in surprise.

"From Richard's Marty?"

Her mother nodded. As she read on, she looked first puzzled, then distressed. Lines of anxiety creased across her forehead.

"He is ill. He has smallpox," she let fall.

Mr. Bemmerton laid down his book and looked up.

"Marty asks us to tell his mother," she told him.

"But we do not know where Margaret is!" he exclaimed.

Richenda's mother returned to the letter.

"The Mistress left us the day after Master Richard was taken ill," she read. "She thought it a low fever. Nought to stay her going."

"Did she not tell Marty her destination?" asked her step-father in shocked surprise.

"Marty sent after her to Richard's grandmother, but she was not there. That is why she has written to us."

Her mother looked so grave that Richenda caught her anxiety.

"Is he very ill?" she asked.

"Smallpox is always a serious illness, my child," her step-father said gently.

Richenda knew how serious it was. Four children in one family had died of it in Benfield last spring.

"But he is strong," said her mother, looking at her steadily over the top of the letter. "We must have faith in God's providence, Richenda."

Richenda could not imagine Richard being ill. He was always so strong and restless and alive. And she could not believe that it was God's will that he should die.

"We must go to them," her stepfather said simply. "Where are they?"

Her mother picked up the letter and frowned at the address.

"The hand is so cramped," she sighed. "I cannot read it. It looks like 'Kissingland'. It can't be that."

"Yes, it can!" exclaimed Richenda. "It's 'Kessingland'— where Marty's sister and her husband live."

"And where's Kessingland?" asked her stepfather.

Richenda shook her head. She did not know. She racked her brains.

"He's a fisherman," she said at last. "I know he's a fisherman because Marty when she was last here said that the chub we ate for dinner tasted like mud in her mouth after the fresh herrings her sister's husband brought home in his boat."

As she spoke, she saw that her parents looked graver and graver.

"So Margaret has left him in a fisherman's hovel," exclaimed her mother in pained surprise.

"By the sea," added Mr. Bemmerton more calmly. "It must be by the sea. But which sea?"

"The North Sea," replied her mother absently. "Marty is a Suffolk woman; you can tell it by her speech."

If her parents were shocked that Richard's mother had left him ill in a hovel, Richenda was appalled that she should have left him at all.

"I *hate* Richard's mother," she burst out suddenly.

So angry was she that she clenched her teeth and stamped her foot.

Her words exploded in the room like so many muskets. In the silence that followed, her mother looked at her sternly.

"Richenda, you must ask God to forgive you."

Her stepfather took her gently by the shoulders.

"The Lord told us to love one another, my child."

But she tore herself away from him in a passion.

"I am sure he also told us to love our children," she burst out. "And Richard's mother does not love him. She knew that he was ill. And she left him."

She remembered afterwards that her mother had knelt down and held out her arms to her.

"Dear heart, we must not judge. We must not judge," she had said. "Only God can see into the secrets of all hearts."

She had run then into her mother's arms and burst into tears.

"You would not have done so," she had sobbed. "You and my father would not have left me had I been ill."

As old Mr. Bemmerton's coach lumbered its slow way through Buckinghamshire and Bedfordshire and over Newmarket Heath on its long journey east towards the Suffolk coast, Richard was asking the same question as Richenda.

He was terribly ill. He could remember even in manhood the black horror that crowded close about him in that dark attic chamber and Marty's anxious face peering at him out of a cloud. He could remember lying in her arms—a great baby of a boy—clinging to her in a torment of fever and fear, feeling himself rejected by all the world save her.

Where was his mother, he cried. Why was she not with them? Why had she left them—now, when he was so ill?

In the listlessness that followed, he lay thinking of his broken childhood, hearing always the thunder and slow drawl of the breakers on the beach below. Ever since he could remember, his mother and old Marty and he had moved from one lodging to the next—at a moment's notice, without rhyme or reason, save for his mother's caprice. And, as often as not, she had not been with them. She had been away in London—or he knew not where. She had been away from them for months. And with no master in the family for them to turn to, he and Marty had often felt frighteningly adrift.

Then, he had let his mind linger happily on that golden afternoon at Maplehampden which had been so different from the rest, and he had seen himself back in the dusty loft above the mill wheel with Thomas and Richenda. Yet even this brought him pain in the end, for he saw how rich both his friends were in those very things that he most bitterly lacked. They had a place in the world; they had a home. Thomas had a father; Richenda had kind Mr. Bemmerton and a mother who was loving and good. Whereas he . . .

"Marty," he begged one quiet morning about a week after the crisis of his illness was past. "Marty, tell me again about my father."

It was a tale he clung to in that long illness.

And the old nurse, understanding his need, had gathered up her sewing and had come and sat beside him in the narrow shaft of sunlight that fell through the tiny cottage window.

His father, she said, had been the most open, generous, and modest young man that ever she had known. The very flower of gentlehood. Strong, very strong, in his faith.

"Tell me about his faith," he said languidly.

Marty wrinkled up her brow in distress. She could explain more clearly what a man *did* than what made him do it. She was a past mistress of fact, but all at sea with abstractions.

"He fought for his right," she stumbled. "For the rights of us all—to be ruled by good English gentlemen sitting in Parliament. Not by a pack of puffed-up prelates and a Popish queen."

He had long seen the struggle for their freedom coming, she said, and he had prepared himself eagerly for the day of battle.

"Why, lamb," Marty said, "I can see thy father now—not more than a boy—shooting at a mark all day with his guns and pistols and his crossbow. And when it rained too hard for him to be out at the target, then would he and Richenda's father, young Richard Bradford, be up in the greater chamber together at their sword-play. Cut and thrust. Cut and thrust. Lord! Lord! How their swords clashed."

He had mortgaged the house at Atheldene and sold his fields to raise his company of men. Six score of them. Men from his own estates. And they had ridden away north to fight the king, cantering two by two through the narrow Sussex lanes, their drums beating, their breastplates gleaming, and their green scarves fluttering in the wind.

It was a brave story she had to tell, and, while she told it, Richard grew richer in his own esteem, seeing that he, too, had a heritage.

His father, she continued, had fought bravely at Edgehill and had retired from it wounded in his sword arm. And he had fought with courage and with hopes undimmed through the long Parliament defeats which followed. It was a terrible time. Wild Royalist bands had been roaming the countryside, setting fire to the Roundhead homesteads left unguarded in the rear, and Richard's mother, left behind in Sussex, had been in great danger from the foe.

"Thy mother was but seventeen at the time," Marty went on. "With thy sister—that died after—a babe at her breast. And thy father came to her over the downs by moonlight through the enemy lines and took us—thy mother and the child and me —down to the coast while it was yet dark and bespoke a fishing boat that carried us to Dover."

Looking back on that scene in the fisherman's cottage as a grown man, Richard could laugh at his foolishness as a boy, for when Marty had told him of that moonlight ride, he had lain still in his bed and closed his eyes, seeing his father galloping over the shadowy turf and snatching up—not his mother—but a fair-haired girl in a quaint net cap. Yet, at other times, when he had opened his eyes and stared at the truth, he had known clearly that it had been his cold, unloving mother whom his father had rescued—not a beautiful, grown-up Richenda. He had known, too, that it had been in his mother's arms that his father had died.

The knowledge had bewildered him beyond bearing.

"It was in the winter of the great snow . . ." Marty said sorrowfully.

Word had come to them at their lodgings in London that Captain Holder had been wounded at the second siege of Arundel. Not a grave wound.

"Then, near the end of that bitter January month," continued Marty, "he sent for thy mother himself. He was ill of the siege fever. He was dying."

The roads round London were choked with snow; and farther south, in Surrey, the thaw had come and the floods were out across the way.

"To go was a great difficulty for thy mother," she said. "For she was great with child—with thee."

Yet the two women had set out on that terrible journey—alone.

It was early in the morning, Marty said, when they at last drove into the shattered town of Arundel. The windows of the houses were broken by the great guns, and the soldiers were stabling their horses in the shops. It was a pitiful sight. From the war-choked ditches rose a pitiful smell.

"But, my father . . ." Richard had interrupted impatiently.

He was sick of hearing about the wars. His father was all his care.

His father was waiting for them, she said, sitting in the window of his chamber, watching the road, his crossbow in his hand.

"His crossbow? But you said he was dying!"

The manner of his father's death always astonished him as a boy.

His father's companions had not been able to keep him in his bed, Marty explained. For three whole days—all the time that the women had been on the journey to him—he had fought his way to the window and leaned there, desperately ill, shooting randomly into the tops of the bare orchard trees and watching the street below, waiting, waiting for the first glimpse of his wife.

"He loved thy mother more than anything in the world," Marty said.

For Richard, Marty's tale was ended. His father was to sit there always in the window at Arundel, waiting for them to come, his crossbow in his hand. He saluted him there. He saluted his father in his dying—all his life.

But what of his mother?

Whenever Richard thought of his mother in that scene at Arundel, he felt achingly confused.

"It was thy mother persuaded thy father back to his bed," said Marty, finishing her tale. "And he lay there in her arms till that terrible siege fever glazed his eyes."

His mother had loved his father. She had given her only son his name: Richard Posthumous Holder. She had even mourned his father's death in his name. And yet, she did not love that son. She did not care for him as Mrs. Bemmerton cared for Richenda, or even reprove and chastise him as Sir James did Thomas.

He was nothing to his mother.

Three days later, while Mr. Bemmerton was driving his old-fashioned coach down the last green lanes, Richard, lying bored in bed, suddenly decided that he was himself again.

The sun was shining; the wind had dropped; and the sea was making the quietest of scraping and jingling sounds as the receding waves scooped back their tribute of small, wet stones. One could hardly hear the sea at all for the crying of the gulls.

"Marty," he shouted down the cottage stairs. "I am better. Fetch my cloak. I am going to sit by the sea."

It was like throwing corn to a barnyard of hens. Marty and her sister and a neighbor set up such a shrill clamor of protest that even the gulls were dumb. But he had his way. Feeling light in the head and at least six feet tall, he shambled weakly

out onto the beach and sat down with his back to the dunes.

It was early November and a day of infinite blue. And, as he sat there, staring first at the wide sweep of the sea and then up into the cloudless, dazzling sky, drawing great breaths of cold, faintly fishy air into his lungs, he was filled with an overwhelming thankfulness for being alive. Everything delighted him—from the whiteness of the gulls' breasts and the fierce greed in their yellow eyes as they swooped on the fish offal strewn about the shingle to the squat ugliness of Marty's brother-in-law's boat drawn far up above the tide, and the litter of lobster pots and corks and tackle. It was life. He loved everything about it. It smelled of pitch and sand and salt and rotting fish. He loved its smell.

Everything that he saw that morning seemed to him exactly right. When Marty's brother-in-law, Jonas, came out of the filthy turf hut where his wife daily gutted his catch, he straightened his back and stared at the sea in just the right way. And then he stumped off noisily towards his boat, crunching the shingle under his boots. He walked like a free man: sturdy and careless and lord of his world. Richard watched him lazily as he sorted his tackle.

"I'll tell him to take me out fishing when I feel better," he thought.

Yet "tell" was not quite the right word. He realized that. He would have to "ask" Jonas Foulger. That was what he would have to do.

So lazy and drugged was he with the joy of being alive that when he saw four horses a long way off, pulling a coach along the sea-shore, he could think only of the beauty of the horses' hoofs flying over the wet sand and of the fun the people in the coach were having, bowling along by the water's edge. And when the coach stopped outside Marty's sister's cottage and he saw Richenda jump down and run inside—ahead of her parents —he thought:

"That's Richenda. That's the Bemmertons. It's strange that they're here at Kessingland instead of at Benfield, where they belong."

And then, into his fuddled mind, darted an unbelievable idea.

They had come to find *him*.

He tottered to his feet and stood wrapped up in the cloak, looking like a scarecrow.

"Richenda! Mrs. Bemmerton! I'm here," he screeched.

He sounded as hoarse as a gull.

Richenda, with all the foreboding of the long journey behind her, heard his strange cry and, turning on her heel in the dark cottage, ran out towards him, standing gaunt and alone on the sunlit beach.

"Richard! Richard!" she shouted.

Voices rose behind her. Warning voices. Marty's. And her mother's.

"Richenda! Richenda, stop!"

But she ran on without heeding. For Richard was alive. He was waiting for her.

"Oh Richard . . ." she panted as she ran towards him. "I thought . . . I thought you might be dead."

There were only three yards of sand between them when Richard awoke to her danger.

"Don't! Don't come any nearer!" he shrieked. "I've been ill."

He knew how ill he had been and how dangerous the illness, for as soon as Marty had seen the pustules that had come out all over his face and body they had all cried in anguish. And then a silence had come upon the cottages. Marty's sister's neighbor had sent away her children.

"I've had smallpox. Don't come near me."

Mrs. Bemmerton caught up with her and flung her arms about her to stop her daughter's flight.

"Richard, dear Richard," she said gently over the top of Richenda's head. "We are so glad you are better."

Richenda could not think how her mother could say he was "better." He looked dreadful. He was as shrunken as a dried-up parsnip; his cheeks were all blotchy; his hair hung in ropes; and his eyes were as large as an owl's.

"We've come to take you home," she burst out. "You and Marty. Home to Benfield."

"As soon as you are stronger," said her mother.

"As soon as the doctor says it is safe for you to travel," said her stepfather, who had joined them.

Their words coming across the stretch of sand to him were like water to a thirsty man. He thought he could never drink his fill.

"Thou art cold," said Marty. "Come thou to bed, child. Thy friends will wait for thee to mend."

She came across the sand and stooped as though to pick him up. But he was not a baby anymore. His illness was past. He was himself.

He threw her off weakly.

"I can walk by myself," he said with a flash of pride. "I am not a child."

※

Richenda never forgot the fortnight that she and her parents spent at Kessingland watching Richard throw off his illness and grow strong again, nor the strange difference that the ten feet of sand between them—which her parents had commanded—made to the quality of their friendship. It was as though they talked together always over the top of a high wall: as though a barrier had been set up not just to keep off infection but to curb their childhood affection for each other. And yet, it was not so. Her parents loved Richard. They treated him like their son.

"It will be different when we are at Benfield," she had thought. "When we are home again, we will ride over to Maplehampden and play again with Thomas. It will be as it was before."

But it never was.

For no sooner was Richard well enough to travel than his mother wrote to Marty, sending her money and ordering her to bring the boy up to London to join her immediately. Richenda and her parents travelled back to Oxfordshire sadly—without him.

When Richard came to Benfield again, they were no longer children.

Yet, though she had lost a close companion on the Suffolk beach, she was about to gain another on the banks of the Thames, for no sooner had she and her parents settled themselves back into their quiet ways at Benfield again than Sir James Egerton paid them a short but important morning visit. Richenda was out walking in the lime avenue at the time. The first sharp frost had hardened the ground and she was enjoying the freedom of walking abroad without her clumsy pattens. The air was so still that she could hear the clatter of a single horse a long way off. Now it galloped past the smithy; now past the church.

"A hard rider . . . in a hurry," she thought. "Perhaps there's a new war . . . or there's a fire . . . or someone is dead."

But when the lone rider turned into the Benfield gates and

came thundering up the avenue, she saw that it was only Sir James—his old cloak and the tattered finery on his hat streaming out behind him in a flutter of ribbons and feathers. He was a big man on a big horse. And the ground shook.

He raised his whip in salutation.

"Are your parents within, Richenda?" he shouted.

And when Richenda nodded her head, he spurred his great horse and thundered on towards the house.

Now, Richenda and the Bemmertons were often over at Maplehampden, but it was an event for Sir James to visit them at Benfield.

What could be the matter? she wondered. Had Thomas got smallpox, too?

As she stood listening to the clatter of the hoofs and the echo of that clatter dying away among the frozen hills, she decided to find out. She ran back up the avenue in Sir James's wake, saw that he had tethered his horse to the pillar of the porch, and ran round the shrubbery to the parlor windows. There was no need to wonder where their guest was being received, for one could hear the shut-in booming of his voice through the wall. She stood on tiptoe in the frozen flower-bed and peered through the pane.

Sir James was pacing up and down like a caged lion she had once seen at a London fair. He was far too large for the little room. He was throwing out rumbling growls at her parents each time he turned on his heel—not angry in tone but proudly persuasive, as though he were asking a favor, beneath the dignity of a lion. She sighed with relief. There could be nothing wrong with Thomas, for her mother was smiling gravely and her stepfather was nodding his head.

She had pressed her nose so close to the pane that her breath had steamed up the glass, and, as she raised her hand to wipe away the blur, her mother looked up, saw her, and frowned with annoyance. Then, she rose quickly and left the room.

"Richenda," she said severely, coming out to her in the garden, "you must not spy on your elders."

"I was not spying," she said indignantly. "I was just looking."

"Then do it openly, child," her mother replied tartly. "Come in at the door. And if it is not fitting that you stay with us, then we will send you away."

That was just what she had feared, Richenda thought.

"But to spy through windows and listen at keyholes," she continued, "are despicable and furtive acts."

Richenda was not sure what "furtive" meant, but the tone of her mother's voice brought the color up into her face, and she ran off towards the woods, hurt and bewildered at having been so unexpectedly shamed.

"I'll stay here for hours and hours," she thought angrily, as she climbed up the most difficult tree that she could manage. "I'll stay here till everyone thinks I am dead."

But it was bitterly cold in the tree. Her face and hands began to ache with the cold. And when she heard Sir James stamp out onto the porch twenty minutes later, mount his horse, and clatter away, she slipped down from her branch and sidled quietly into the house for the warmth of the kitchen fire.

Her parents were laughing gently together in the parlor.

"Poor James," her mother was saying. "He should have had Richard for a son—not Thomas."

This seemed such an extraordinary thing for her mother to have said—and, laughingly too, after being so cross—that Richenda burst straight into the room for an explanation.

"Why?" she demanded. "Why should Richard have been Sir James's son—and not Thomas?"

They both looked startled and taken aback.

"Richenda!" her mother began reprovingly, the frown coming back onto her face. "What did I just tell you?"

"I couldn't help it! I really couldn't," she said passionately. "I wasn't listening at keyholes. What you said just came out into the passage as I was walking past."

Her stepfather smiled.

"What does mother mean?" she asked him.

He made her sit beside him on a stool and he then explained to her gently that Sir James found it difficult to understand his son, for Thomas was so quiet and shy and different from his sisters. His son did not like doing the things that he had liked doing as a boy; he did not like rat-catching and throwing the fox to the hounds; he did not like setting one cock fighting upon another.

"Besides," said her mother sadly, "Thomas is afraid of his father's dogs."

"No, he isn't!" Richenda contradicted her hotly. "He just doesn't like the horrible noise they make. Nor do I."

"Besides, Thomas likes books," her stepfather said, smiling. "He wants to spend the day reading."

"And does his father think that is wrong?"

"Thomas has been pestering his father to teach him Latin," put in her mother.

"Then why doesn't he."

A gleam of amusement shot across her stepfather's face.

Her mother explained that this had been the reason for Sir James's visit. Richenda's stepfather had kept up his classical studies rather more zealously than Sir James had done, and he had therefore asked her stepfather to start Thomas on his Latin grammar.

"And will you?" she asked him eagerly.

Old Mr. Bemmerton nodded his head.

"I am going to teach you both together, my dear."

"Me? Are you going to teach *me* Latin, too?"

"We begin tomorrow morning at half-past eight."

Richenda came to look back on those morning lessons with Thomas as one of the happiest times in her childhood. Outside, the mists hung heavy over the Thames valley. And, in the nation at large, those who had sat in judgement on their king and cut off his head now fell to quarrelling bitterly among themselves as each snatched at the reins of power. It was an inglorious time. Yet it was not so at Benfield. Here, in her stepfather's study, there was nothing but light and affection and the excitement of learning.

"We must set to our task with a will," her stepfather had said that first morning, smiling at them both over the top of his glasses. "You are a year late, Thomas, at entering in upon your Latin, so we must work hard to catch up with the boys whom you will join in the spring."

For Thomas was to go away to a grammar school the next April. That had been decided upon from the beginning.

"But that is what I wish, sir," replied Thomas with his shy smile.

He was in such a quiver of impatience to begin that he could scarcely sit still and keep quiet that first hour, while old Mr. Bemmerton cut them both their pens.

"You will have to do this for yourselves in time," he told them. "So watch carefully what I am doing."

But Thomas's eyes kept straying into the pages of Lily's Grammar.

"What does *Diluculo surgere saluberrimum est* mean?" he asked.

"In time. In time," her stepfather replied, choosing a strong, straight quill with maddening care.

Richenda always smiled ever after when someone exclaimed, "In time. In time," for Mr. Bemmerton was always saying it in the next few months. For Thomas tore into his studies as though he had been starving for knowledge all his life. Richenda was amazed. He continually astonished her. In his eagerness to learn, he forgot himself entirely. He forgot that he was shy and small and disregarded. He forgot everything but what was inside the books in front of his eyes. He even forgot Richenda herself.

"Oh, Father, do make Thomas stop," she would say irritably at times. "I can't keep up."

While, deep inside herself, she would mourn that she was only a very ordinary sort of girl and that Thomas was turning out an eagle.

Yet, being Thomas, he was not cruel or proud—as an eagle is. He was only excited and happy.

"What happens next?" he would ask eagerly when her stepfather closed the pages on his daily reading to them from Chapman's translation of the *Iliad*. "Does Achilles beat Hector? Oh, please go on, sir. Please go on."

While he was with Mr. Bemmerton his shyness dropped from him utterly. He seemed quite a different person. Yet, sometimes, the two Thomases would appear at one and the same moment sitting opposite her on the far side of the study table.

One such occasion she remembered all her life.

Thomas had been racing far ahead of her in his Latin grammar and had even—for once—in a way overshot his own comprehension.

"You must not rush your fences, my boy," said her stepfather. "Take your time. Take your time. Of course you will fall if you try to clear a gate before you have learned to jump."

Both Richenda and Thomas went scarlet with grief.

"Is it the same thing?" Thomas whispered, the old hurt and puzzlement back in his eyes.

"What's the same thing?" asked Mr. Bemmerton in concern.

"Jumping a real gate?"

Richenda had been present when Sir James had shouted at his son only the afternoon before for falling off his horse in front of a gate.

"Thomas, you're a milksop and a coward," he had yelled.

"Both need courage and experience, my boy," replied her stepfather, smiling gravely. "You have the courage. It is the knowledge how to do it that you lack."

Meanwhile, Richard was learning his lessons in a harder school.

His mother had married again. She had married a dismal, weary-looking Presbyterian widower called Philip Drew. Such a thunderclap was enough to frighten a boy out of his childhood forever.

When he and Marty had come up from Suffolk, his mother had taken no pity on their tiredness or his own evident debility after his grave illness, but had taken them up to a gloomy room in the strange London house and there—without more ado— had presented them both to their new master.

"Philip," she said, turning to a grim old man seated in a tall chair. "This is my son."

Then she turned to Richard.

"Kneel, my son," she said. "And ask your father for his blessing."

His father!

He could have cried aloud with pain.

His *father!* But his father had ridden out from Atheldene in the morning of the world. His father had been strong and brave. Marty had told him so. Somehow, rebellious and wretched as he was, he found his way down to his knees and, kneeling there, felt too stunned even to be sickened by his stepfather's sour old age. Yet that pierced him, too, in the end, for as he rose to his feet with the blessing bestowed, it shot through him that he could have forgiven his mother if she had married an old man like Mr. Bemmerton. Richenda's stepfather was grave and gentle and smelled of tobacco. It came to him that he could have endured a stepfather who was healthy and whole.

"He is older than I thought," said his stepfather, eyeing him critically.

Clearly, he liked Richard no better than Richard liked him. Indeed, they hated each other at first sight.

"He is nearly eight years old, Philip," said his mother.

"Ah, then," he smiled thinly, "he should be in his Mantuan."

Richard remembered that he was very puzzled by this. What was a "Mantuan," he wondered. He remembered thinking that it must be some sort of coat that he ought to be wearing now that he was nearly eight and that his mother had been too poor or too negligent to buy him one.

"He knows no Latin, I think," replied his mother, looking embarrassed.

Mr. Drew frowned at him deeply, accounting his ignorance a great sin, he could see.

"He is backward, Margaret," he said severely. "Very backward for his age."

"He can read his Bible in good English, sir," burst out Marty indignantly. "He knows his Commandments and his duty to God and his duty to his neighbor. That's enough as is meet for a child."

"Be quiet, woman!" whipped out his stepfather in a voice that cut like a lash. "Thou know'st nothing of the training of a gentleman."

To Marty, who had nursed Richard's father, this was almost beyond bearing. She bridled up and went red in the face like an angry turkey cock.

"I'll take myself to the servants, mistress," she said bitterly to his mother and stumped out of the room, so mortified that she quite forgot what kind of scene she was leaving Richard to endure in that hateful room.

His new father called him to his knee and put him through an inquisition more fitting for a heretic on the rack or a thief at the bar than for a child of seven but recently recovered from the smallpox.

Did his new son know how to make his quill and to write? he asked. Could he cipher and do simple accounts? Had he learned the use of the globes? At each question Richard grew more and more ashamed of his ignorance. He had none of these arts.

To tell the truth, his mother looked ashamed, too.

"Why, then," rasped Mr. Drew, "let me search you in your Bible."

Richard shifted his feet uneasily. He knew the exciting parts of the Old Testament—like David killing Goliath with a stone; and the story of Samson; and the tale of the she-bear eating up the children who had mocked Elisha—but Marty and he had left pages and pages of the Holy Book unread because they had thought they looked dusty and dull.

"Come, boy, hold up your head. Tell me the name of Abraham's wife?"

Richard stared at his stepfather wretchedly and counted three white hairs sprouting out of the mole on his cheek.

The old man tapped his fingers irritably on the arms of his chair. "How many children had Adam and Eve?"

Richard stood before his stepfather feeling as stupid as a mule.

"Have you never heard of Abel, dolt?"

"Yes, sir," he gasped, suddenly perceiving a plank to save him in the raging sea of his ignorance.

"Tell me about him, then."

"Abel has yellow hair and a very red face," he began triumphantly. "He can whistle through his teeth and he's very good with the horses."

"What are you saying?" shrieked his stepfather.

Richard turned to his mother in horror, not understanding at all why the old man was so enraged.

"Abel Fitch is his grandmother's groom, Philip," she said faintly. "He taught the boy to ride."

Mr. Drew threw up his hands in despair.

"Your son, Margaret, is a perfect barbarian!" he exclaimed.

When he had calmed himself somewhat, he fell to lecturing them both severely on the extent of Richard's backwardness. Not only had the boy failed to learn the very little that he had been taught but he had also fallen far behind his contemporaries in the more formal subjects of a gentleman's education. The child was nearly two years behind in his schooling, he said. He should have begun studying Lily's Grammar when he was six and have read through Cato's *Distichs* and his Latin Testament before he was seven.

"And Greek!" he rasped shrilly. "He should have started his Greek!"

Richard remembered that the dreary man began wheezing and sighing over his lack of learning like the east wind blowing up for a gale in the Kessingland elms.

"We must send him to school," he concluded at last. "We have not a moment to lose."

And so, to school Richard had gone—glad in his heart to be separated from a mother whom he could neither understand nor forgive and from the man whom she called her husband.

At school, he was at least on his own.

3
❊ Schooldays

YET why he had been sent to Wittendon Free Grammar School before all other schools in the country, Richard could not well understand. Nor—since his knowledge of England at the time was curiously muddled and uninformed—was he sure where this same town of Wittendon rightly stood. He could see hills out of the school window, crowned with trees; and where a farmer had tried to plow the stony ground, the furrow gleamed grayish-white. There was a bakery in Wittendon Street at which he bought tarts on half-holidays; and there was a smithy hard by the gibbet at the cross-roads. When they went to church to listen to the sermons, he saw that its walls were stuck with flints—like the churches in Suffolk. That was all that he knew about the town of his schooling in the first few months.

And then, one sunlit April afternoon, he learned more.

It was at the time when the travelling penman came to instruct the boys in their writing. Richard was standing by the master's desk, his pen-knife and his goose quill in his hands, learning to cut his nib slantwise to the breadth of a barley-corn, when on looking up and glancing through the great window of the Free School he saw two blurred figures, one small, one large, walking across the school yard towards the master's house. Because of the bottle glass of some of the lower panes, they were strangely pulled out sideways, like faces seen in the bowl of a spoon. And, being hare-witted and easily amused, he grinned at the sight.

"Another poor fool being dragged to school," he thought.

And then—wonder of all wonders—as the figures came to the panes that were clear and true, Thomas emerged, tugging Sir James Egerton up the steps to the master's door.

"It's Thomas!" he exclaimed aloud. And then, watching his friend's eagerness to come to school, he shouted:

"Thomas, you simpleton!"

"Nay!" roared the penman, giving Richard's ear a cruel tweak. " 'Tis thou art the simpleton, thou clumsy boy."

His knife had slipped and he had spoiled his pen.

It was less than six months since he and Richenda and Thomas had walked over the perilous weir bridge, but so much had happened to Richard in the meantime that Thomas seemed to him like a friend from his distant past.

"It is good to be at school, I think," said Thomas shyly at their first meeting in the yard.

"No. It is not good," he replied sharply. "It is tedious. You will soon find it so."

Poor Thomas! he thought. He is still only a child. He knows nothing of the world.

Then, suddenly, he wished they were all three back at Maplehampden again.

"I am glad you have come," he told Thomas. "I had never thought to see you again."

With the catastrophe of his mother's remarriage, he had banished all hopes of meeting anyone from Benfield. Richenda had, surely, vanished from his life forever.

"But how comes it that your father has sent you to Wittendon?" he asked his friend.

"It is the nearest good school to my father's house," replied Thomas.

"To Maplehampden?"

"Yes. It is but a ten-mile ride over the hills. I hope they will come to me often."

Maplehampden! And if near Maplehampden, near Benfield, too!

"In which direction?" asked Richard eagerly.

Thomas turned himself round, as puzzled whence he had come as an acorn dropped from an oak. Then, scanning the shape of the hills beyond the Wittendon chimney-pots, he suddenly pointed west.

"That was the way we came," he said. "Yes. That was the way. My father and I rode down that woodland track. We crossed the common where the sheep are grazing."

Richard gazed upwards at a westering cloud sailing across the April blue, high above the bare beech trees on top of the hills, and rejoiced to think that Richenda might be able to see the same cloud if she happened to strain her eyes eastward.

"How is she?" he asked.

"Who?"

"Richenda?" he shouted angrily.

He did not know why he felt so angry—unless it was because he had kept Richenda so long locked up inside himself—thinking about her as she had been on the Suffolk beach; talking to her; imagining himself saving her from all sorts of dreadful harms—that now he could not bear to let her name out of his mouth into the shouting bedlam of the school yard.

"She is well," replied Thomas shortly, hurt by his anger.

"Tell me more."

"She is quick at her Latin."

"At her Latin?" exclaimed Richard in surprise. He did not know that girls ever learned Latin. "How do you know she is quick?"

His desperate possessiveness made his voice sound hoarse with anger.

"Because we have had lessons together."

Thomas turned away from Richard, the tears big in his eyes. All his life he heard what people meant rather than what they said. And he must have understood Richard's unkindness that day at their new meeting better than Richard understood it himself.

Looking at Thomas and seeing the crestfallen angle of his

head, Richard was overcome with remorse. His heart felt heavy as a falling stone. Thomas had come to him with childlike trust. He had come as a friend.

"Thomas, Thomas," he cried, catching up with him. "I am so glad that you have come."

They never mentioned Richenda's name at school after that. Yet their memory of her remained as an unspoken bond between them, setting them apart from the other boys—who did not even know that she existed. This and their affection for each other bound them together when all else in their school lives might have swept them in opposite directions.

For Thomas was a born scholar. At Maplehampden he had seemed to Richard just another boy—more thoughtful, perhaps, and less rash than he—but a person as imprisoned in childhood as Richenda and himself. At school, however, he watched his friend outsoar their childish world in a matter of weeks. Before he was nine Thomas had torn through his Latin and Greek grammar and was gambolling about in Aesop's *Fables* and Mantuan and Terence and Ovid like a young horse turned out into a spring meadow. Richard and the rest of the boys would have knocked him over the head had he been less modest and less innocently surprised by his own gifts. But, as it was, he was so willing to share the fruits of his knowledge with others and so quiet and friendly that he stole their hearts. They were proud of him. They were proud that their school could produce such a boy. And, because of this, they forgave him his white face and his great owl eyes and his puny pair of fists.

As for Richard, he was no fool. He learned what was put before him grimly and well. He had no choice. His stepfather had told him bluntly upon his setting out to school that he would educate him as a gentleman for as long as the master said that he prospered in his studies, but that should he once fail he would apprentice him to a merchant and have done with him. Richard was a burden to him, he knew. His father's estates were mortgaged, and a large part of them were disputed by another. Atheldene itself had been burned to the ground.

"You have nothing to inherit," his stepfather said, "but your father's name—and his debts."

There was scorn in his voice. And Richard—being young then in the ways of the world—had fallen into a passion that his father, who had given his all in the Parliament cause, should be so slighted by such a dreary skinflint of an old man.

"My father was a hero, sir," he had cried out in anger.

"Then let me not see his son fall into beggary and disgrace," whipped out Mr. Drew.

Beggary and disgrace, indeed!

It suited Richard ill to be an apprentice; but the thought that he might one day be a beggar and disgraced put him into a perfect panic. The boys at Wittendon Free Grammar School knew about beggars. The town lay on the high road through the hills. And Richard had but to sit on the wall of the school yard at certain times of the year to see droves of vagabonds and rogues: ragged Royalist soldiers maimed in the wars, and barefoot, crazy people with long hair, prophesying the end of the world, passing through the Chilterns on their way to the great country fair. They were a terror to ordinary folk, these wild, penniless, evil-smelling travellers of the road. And, looking down upon them from his school wall, he had no wish to join their flock. Therefore, he gritted his teeth, worked as hard at his books as was needful, and endured the long ignominy of being beaten into a gentleman, thinking—as well he might— that there were worse places in the world than school.

Yet his heart was not in what he was taught. It was almost everywhere else instead. His eyes were out of the window watching the swallows, while his mind wondered where they had been all the winter long. His nose sniffed the sweet scent of hay and the dry, sharp prickle of harvest dust, while he puzzled hard that a tiny mote or speck snuffed up one's nostrils should make the whole of one's body explode in a sneeze. He wondered, too, why the sunlight falling through the cracked window-pane in the Wittendon church nave broke into orange and violet and green, while elsewhere—through the uncracked glass —it shone as sunlight should. Where did the colors come from?

he asked. He asked a hundred other questions as well. Why, for example, did plums and apples fall *down* from the tree and not *upwards* into the sky? And why—most astonishing of all—when he walked down Wittendon Street could he see the blacksmith at work in his forge strike the horseshoe on his anvil seconds before he caught the clang of his hammer?

The master used to answer impatiently that it *was* so, and that Richard was wasting his time considering such trifles.

"You might as well ask, young fool, why the sky is blue."

Well, why is it blue? he asked himself. Why not black or purple or green?

The other boys, too, thought him a fool to question such things.

Only Thomas—true and kind in his friendship—bore with him and tried to puzzle out the answers.

"As for the swallows," he said, "I think they go into the bottom of rivers in the winter. That's why we don't see them."

"You mean that they live under the water?" Richard exclaimed incredulously.

"Well, I think they sleep there."

Many animals slept through the winter months, he explained. Hedgehogs did. They made a nest of dead leaves.

"But, Thomas," said Richard, beginning to jeer, "how can a bird live under water? He could not breathe."

But Thomas stuck to his point. He had watched the swallows at Maplehampden only last autumn. They had gathered in flocks and then skimmed over the surface of the Thames, not once but again and again. He had seen them dip their beaks into the water, he said.

"They were trying it out—just as we do with our toes before we swim."

And next morning the swallows were gone.

"So I think they must have gone down to the bottom of the river to sleep."

That first September at Wittendon, Richard and Thomas watched the swallows gathering in the trees above the school yard.

Beyond the wall at the back stretched a large pond.

"Come and see," shouted Thomas one morning.

Richard joined him on the wall and saw for himself that the swallows skimmed over the surface of the water again and again, seeming to kiss it and so sending tiny ripples out in widening rings.

Two days later the birds had gone.

"There's only one way to prove it," Richard said.

"What's that?"

"Dive in and look for them," he replied.

It was a filthy pond, mantled with green duckweed and buzzing with flies.

"The master will beat us," said Thomas, shivering but not dismayed.

"If we go early enough in the dawn," Richard said, "he will not know."

And so, early next morning, they crept out of their attic dormitory in their night-shifts and climbed the school wall. It was cold to their bare feet, for the dew was heavy on the grass.

"Take off your shift," Richard whispered, pulling his own off over his head.

They stood there in their nakedness, shivering in the cold dawn. Thomas's teeth were chattering loud in his head.

"Slip in quietly," he said. "We'd best make no noise."

And so they crept into that disgusting, muddy pond and, taking a deep breath, forced their heads under the mantling green and opened their eyes in a murky gloom of long, waving weeds and darting small fish.

Ten seconds later they came up choking for air.

"We must get right down to the bottom. That's where they'll be," panted Thomas, almost blue in the face with the cold.

So down they went again to the mud and to the rubbish that the boys had thrown over the wall. Richard saw a worn-out shoe and a broken school slate. There was even a great cannonball down there, shot into the pond, he supposed, during the Wittendon siege.

But never a sleeping swallow did either of them see.

"They have built themselves nests in the mud already. That's why we could not see them," explained Thomas as the two of them rolled in the grass to let the dew clean the slime off their bodies.

"Holder! Egerton!" roared the master from the top of the wall. "What the devil have you been at?"

Yet even the great beating they both got did not stop Richard from asking questions or Thomas from trying to answer them.

They were much puzzled a year later about witches. Could old women really cast spells on their neighbors' cows so that their milk dried up and the creatures fell down sick and died? Thomas did not know. He had never met a witch. But he supposed that if good people like Elijah and Elisha could work miracles, then bad people like witches could work evil.

"But the Lord helped Elijah and Elisha," Richard objected. "Do you think He helps the witches, too?"

This was a great problem to them both. For the Lord had created the world and all that was in it. And so—since there was wickedness in the world—He must have created that, too.

Thomas was troubled over this problem for months and months. He wrestled with it at sermon time, when he ought to have been getting the text and the argument by heart, ready to turn into Latin sentences next day. The thought that God might have created the Devil made him quite ill, Richard remembered years later. The anxiety of it troubled his dreams so that he cried out loud in his sleep. As for Richard himself, he soon tired of such abstractions. He wanted to know much simpler and more immediate things. He wanted to know how something as beautiful and fragile as a butterfly ever came to be shut up in a hard and ugly chrysalis.

Richard's curiosity was often foolish. He asked questions at this time as readily as another boy might boast or tell lies. And the habit made him ridiculous among his companions. They used to get him into a corner of the school yard and chant jeeringly:

Here stands nosey Richard Holder
Quot? Quo modo? Ubi? Cur?

The taunt had him two ways—for he had inherited from his father a nose as long as the Devil's. He was proud of his nose, knowing whence it came. And he would lash out at his tormentors with his fists and kick at their legs and trip them up till he and they were all down in a struggling heap of arms and legs.

Yet his ungovernable inquisitiveness at school brought him the one piece of good fortune he was ever to have in those long years at Wittendon—the one piece of good fortune in his life.

It was this way.

On their half-holidays Richard would often wander alone about Wittendon, poking his long nose into the many workshops of the place, watching the wheelwright and the saddler and the potter at their work, for it always gave him a strangely pleasant shiver up the length of his spine to watch a man making something with skill. His greatest joy was in the smithy. He spent long hours watching Mr. Roades beat out horseshoes and plowshares and twist the red-hot iron into fire-dogs and turnspits and such like things. He came so often that at last the blacksmith grunted that Richard might help him with the bellows. And he—nothing loath—leaped to the task, at once proud and happy that he had been asked to be of service to so skilful a man.

He was there in the smithy blowing the bellows one bitter December afternoon in the year 1655, when a traveller stopped for the frosting of his horse's hoofs. The task was a long one, for the shoes needed roughening and nailing so that the horse would not slip on the ice-bound ways. And the traveller stood by the forge, watching Richard and Mr. Roades at their task. His face was caught in the light of the coals. Richard saw that he had a wide, deep brow, an eye as bright as a gallipot, and a nose even longer than his own. It was not a face to forget. He puzzled Richard greatly, for he had the speech of a gentleman and yet he wore the shabbiest and most old-fashioned coat that Richard had ever seen. It was fitter for a beggar than for the scholar and philosopher that he soon proved to be.

"Blacksmith," he said, having observed Richard as inquisitively as Richard had observed him. "Methinks your apprentice has a sharp look to his eye. Doth he study your trade as keenly as he studies your customers' faces, eh?"

Richard blushed at having been caught in his staring, while Mr. Roades grunted that Richard was no apprentice of his, but a boy from the grammar school who liked to be playing about the forge when he was free from his master and his books.

"And why like you the forge?" asked the traveller.

"Because, sir," he answered readily enough, "Mr. Roades is a good blacksmith. I like to watch him work. I like the things he makes."

The stranger digested this piece of information thoughtfully, while Richard chattered on. He was always at ease with strangers.

"Besides, sir, I am puzzled by fire."

"How's that?" pounced the traveller, his great nose seeming to bear down on Richard like a ship's prow.

"Why, sir, I marvel that it burns wood, melts metal, boils water, but that if you cast a stone in the coals it goes black and then bursts asunder."

"The devil!" exclaimed Mr. Roades in surprise.

Indeed, his experiment with a great Chiltern flint that he had lugged there from the hills had been kept secret from the blacksmith. He had done it when Mr. Roades had gone home to drink his ale.

"Tell me more," commanded the stranger, fixing him with his piercing eye. "What else have you discovered?"

Richard looked inwards over the huge desert of his ignorance.

"Not much," he said frankly.

The man smiled and then asked:

"What other things puzzle you, then?"

Richard looked at him narrowly. Was he making fun of him? he wondered. Or was he in earnest? No grown-up—except Mr. Bemmerton—had ever taken his questions seriously before. Yet the man's voice was not sarcastic; his eyes did not mock.

Richard told him, tentatively, about the sunlight pouring through the cracked pane in the Wittendon church and of the splash of purple and orange and green that it made on the floor of the nave.

The stranger nodded his head.

"Go on," he said.

And then, since the man had not laughed at him, Richard poured out the sum of his puzzlement.

"And sir, is it not strange," he gabbled on, "that when we eat an egg it is naught but yolk and white, and yet if a hen sits on it for but three weeks there is a chick burst out of the shell with a head and eyes and a beak and soft claws?"

This delighted the traveller. He suddenly smiled.

"Why boy," he burst out, "so I wondered when I was a boy!"

He told Richard that he had kept a hen on a clutch of eggs in his room at Oxford and that he had taken one of the eggs every three days and smashed its shell and studied what was within.

"And what did you find?" Richard asked eagerly.

"Why, that the chicken came very slowly to itself within the shell—little bit by little bit—till it was ready to peck its way out."

Then, forgetting the mystery of the birth of chickens, the stranger bombarded Richard with questions about himself as fiercely as his stepfather had done four years ago when they had first met. Yet this stranger was fierce not because he wished to confound him but because he was quick and impatient in his mind, wishing to get at things in haste. Had Richard begun his studies in algebra and geometry? he asked. No? And he made a

short cluck in his throat. Had he learned aught of the stars?
No? Was he interested in anatomy? Richard did not know
what the word "anatomy" rightly meant; but when the stranger
had explained, he said "Yes." He was interested in anatomy.
Then, said the man, had he ever heard of Dr. Harvey's great
discovery of the circulation of the blood?

"No," said Richard. And he begged him to explain it to him.

Mr. Roades put down his hammer and stared in amazement
as the tattered, shabby old gentleman grasped Richard's right
hand and folded his fingers over his left wrist.

"Now, can you feel your pulse?" he asked.

Richard nodded.

"And now here? And again, here?"

He had closed Richard's fingers first round his left forearm
till he had found again the familiar throb, and he had next
placed their tips gently against the pulse in his neck. Our hearts
were pumps, he said, and it was this pumping of blood from the
heart that Richard felt with his finger-tips. And then he explained how the blood flowed to the very extremities of men's
bodies and then came back again to their hearts.

Richard's delight in this discovery about himself must have
shone in his face, for the traveller smiled back at him almost
tenderly, as though he had been his own son.

Mr. Roades had finished the shoes by now.

"What is your name?" asked the stranger as he mounted his
horse.

Richard told him.

"And who is your father?"

"He is dead, sir."

The traveller asked him then what he planned to do with his
life, which puzzled him greatly, for he had not thought till that
moment that boys could plan what they did with themselves. He
had thought that his stepfather and his mother and his master
at school had power to choose what he did for a career.

"I do not know, sir," he replied.

"Well, Richard Holder," the man said, leaning down to his
saddle-bag and pulling out paper and ink and quill, "here is my

name and address. Should you ever be minded to study natural philosophy further, then write to me and I will help you."

And he was off on the instant up the hill towards London.

Richard looked at the paper and read: "Dr. PHINEAS BOTELER, M.D., Wood Street, Cheapside, London."

He ran back eagerly to tell Thomas of his strange new acquaintance and of what he had told him about their hearts and their blood. And Thomas, to please him, began feeling for his pulse in his wrist and his forearm and his neck, as Richard instructed him. But Richard could see that his mind was not on it.

Thomas had just discovered that he could read Homer without his master's help. And all his thoughts were in front of Troy at the great siege.

4
❖ In the Broken Times

THOSE schooldays at Wittendon seemed never-ending to Richenda, left companionless at Benfield. It was not that she was unhappy with her parents. They surrounded her with love. But—with Thomas gone—she had lost her zest for the many things that they had once done together. There was no one now to smile at her from the other side of the study table or to race her up the next hill of learning. And there was no Richard, either, to dare her to climb the beech trees or to gallop over ditches too wide for their ponies. She felt lonely, left behind—and dull.

"Why do boys have to go away?" she asked her mother pettishly. "What is so special about boys?"

"When they grow up, dear heart, they have to make their way in the world," her mother replied. "They become ministers and lawyers and doctors. . . ."

Then, playfully, she took her daughter's upturned face between her hands. "They even become fathers of little daughters," she added, smiling.

Richenda scowled her tremendous scowl.

And little daughters, she thought savagely, had to learn to sew men's shirts and to count the long hours till they grew up

49

into wives. And, being a wife was tedious, too. In a lightning
flash, she saw her mother's virtuous life stretching out before
her, like a long, narrow road through a flat plain. Her mother
never seemed to amuse herself. She never dawdled or had moments of frantic excitement—as Richenda did. She never in-
dulged in sulks, or burst out singing, or looked as though she
felt like rolling over and over down Hampden Hill. Morning
and night, she knelt at her prayers in the parlor, and all the
hours between she passed from one small, tedious duty to the
next: in the parlor; in the still-room; in the garden; in the village. It seemed to Richenda a monotonous and unrewarding
round, as though her mother—and all women with her—were
condemned from birth to do things only for other people; never
for themselves.

"I wish you and father had not made me a girl," she burst out passionately.

Her mother looked down at her in surprise.

"But, my child, it was not your parents. It was God."

"Then, I wish God had not made me a girl," she said rebelliously.

Mrs. Bemmerton put her finger quickly over her daughter's lips.

"You must not say such things, Richenda," she said sternly. "You must never question God's will. He has His purpose when He makes us what we are."

Then, seeing Richenda's defiance dissolve into unhappiness, she added more tenderly:

"He will reveal His purpose to you, my dear, when you are older. Truly, He will. And then, you will understand what he wants you to do—as a woman."

Yet in the lonely tedium of those schooldays there were always the school holidays.

Richard came to Benfield almost as though it were his home. Indeed, it *was* his home. His mother and stepfather had little use for him in London. They had children now of their own. One, two, three sallow, sickly Drew stepbrothers had been born to him in the space of three years.

"I only add to their burden in Paternoster Row," he confessed cheerfully to Mr. Bemmerton. "Besides, sir, I would much rather be here."

Richard addressed all his remarks to Richenda's stepfather when he first came from Wittendon. It was as though she and her mother were beneath his notice. And this maddened Richenda. She thought him arrogant and rude. He talked endlessly, down the length of the table to the only other man, of the archery exercises they were having at school and about a new way to catch pike and of an old man he had met at the Wittendon smithy who had told him all about the circulation of the blood.

He has not asked one word about what *I* have been doing all this time, she thought bitterly. Or how I am getting on with my lute.

It was always Thomas who brought them together again.

Thomas rode over from Maplehampden as soon as his father gave him permission, jumped off his pony in front of the hall door, threw down his reins, and ran into the house.

"Richenda!" he shouted. "Richenda, where are you?"

And when he had found her he flung his arms round her—quite forgetting that he was now a schoolboy.

"Richenda, you've grown. You've shot up like a willow!"

The long, empty months of his absence rolled away like a mist.

He was so overjoyed at seeing her that she burst out laughing with delight.

"Have you learned those hymn tunes in Alison's book?" he gabbled. "And what about William Lawes? Or was he too difficult, after all?"

And then, laughing and happy, quite forgetful of Richard's neglect, she ran off to fetch her instrument. She played to them self-consciously, at first, eager to show Thomas what she could do. But, at length, the music stole over her. She played for herself alone—lost to the two boys, to the parlor, to Benfield—hardly aware that they were her own fingers that were striking the lute.

At such times, Richard remembered long afterwards, he would look up from whatever he was doing—from making a fly from his rod, or whatever it was—and gaze and gaze at Richenda, released at last by the music from his shyness, and marvel anew that she should be so beautiful.

And when the last chord was struck and the echo of Richenda's voice was swallowed up in silence, he would suddenly leap to his feet.

"Richenda, Thomas, let us go fishing," he would say excitedly. "It is months and months since we tried that reach below Hampden Hill."

And, with a single magic touch on Time's wheel, they were back again where they had been before.

❈

Why were those weeks of the holidays so short? Why did they ever waste a single hour of them quarrelling among themselves?

Why do people never realize that they are happy in the moments that they are so? Richenda used to ask herself years later, at a time of grief.

They were given such a short time in which to be glad, and Richard wasted whole mornings of it, proving to himself that he was the stronger and the better man. This urge of his to excel—and to be acknowledged as excelling—vexed her dreadfully at the time. It made her feel ashamed of him.

Yet, she understood it, too.

"He is like me," she used to think. "We both want to win."

Realizing this, she saw that she understood her old childhood playmate far better than she understood Thomas.

"It's as though Richard and I were twins," she thought ruefully, after one of their bitterest quarrels. "It's as though we shared more than our Christian names."

Her own early gladness was clouded over towards the middle of her fifteenth year. She could not put a date to her unhappiness and say, "Yesterday I was joyful; today I am not," for the damp that came about her crept down slowly like a cold fog. Little by little, the sun was shorn of its rays, and the color faded out of her world. It was September—a month that she had always loved before. But in that September of 1658 she would stand at the Benfield windows and stare at the Chiltern Hills and think how silent and drab and unheeding the beech trees stood. Even the waters of the Thames lay sullen under a sullen sky. What had happened? she wondered. It had always been so beautiful before. She had a terrible feeling that she was saying good-bye to something forever—though she could not think what this something was. She knew only that she ached with unhappiness because the thing was gone.

Nor was this all. For, turning her eyes inwards upon her home, she saw that a light had gone out of Benfield, too. Unwillingly and in misery, she saw her parents with new eyes. She saw that her stepfather was growing old and that, in his decline, he was as unhappy as herself. He was always gentle and considerate and kind, but during their lessons together he fell daily more often into a long abstraction, in which he wrinkled up his brow and sighed and muttered words under his breath as though his soul were wrestling in anguish with an adversary. In their family prayers, he no longer thanked God joyfully for his plum crop or that the muck-spreading had been done so quickly and well. Instead, he besought Him desperately for forgiveness—always for forgiveness.

But he has never done anything wrong, thought Richenda in deep distress.

Her stepfather had been a living pattern to her of all that was good and happy in men. She could not bear that he should feel sinful.

My mother must comfort him, she thought.

But when she turned her eyes upon her mother, she saw that her mother was always busy with her duties. She had taken on many more in the last few months, for she now managed her husband's small estate at Benfield and—under his direction— also treated with the lawyers and the agent concerning Richenda's own estate in Hampshire, bequeathed her by her father. There was much to do. And her mother did it—with a quiet competence that matched everything else that Richenda had ever known about her.

She is helping him with works, she thought. But my stepfather needs words. He needs to talk about his grief.

With her new insight into her parents, Richenda had grown shy of them. She could no longer say, "Father, what is the matter?" or, "Mother, make him feel happy again," as she could have done only six months before. A barrier stood between them. She felt imprisoned in diffidence. She was beset with doubts. She began to think that her mother lacked imagination or that she wilfully neglected them both for the sake of others.

With all these mortgages and land sales and Gaffer Calcutt's bronchitis and the herbs to be culled for the medicines, she's forgotten about father and me, she thought angrily. It's *us* that want her. She ought to see that.

And then, recognizing clearly what she was thinking, she was overcome with shame, seeing herself as disloyal to a mother whom she had always loved.

Suddenly, in the space of a few weeks, everywhere had lost its joy.

At Maplehampden, things were far worse than they were at Benfield. Life was openly and noisily unhappy.

Richenda had suspected for some time that all was not well. The suspicion had stolen upon her slowly, not through anything that Thomas ever *said,* for he spoke little of his home when he was at Benfield. But his eyes betrayed him. They betrayed him when she played her lute.

Then, all at once, the whole valley from Maplehampden up to Benfield was talking of Sir James's wild and intemperate ways. He galloped nightly over the fields that the Parliament surveyors had taken away from him, firing off his pistol and trampling down the crops that the new Puritan owners had sown upon his father's land. He was seen drunk in his own village in the middle of the day.

"Is Thomas's father mad?" she had asked her stepfather, when they were alone together at their Virgil.

Mr. Bemmerton had looked grave and thoughtful. He took so long to answer that Richenda wondered whether he had fallen into another of his abstractions.

"Not mad, child," he said at last. "Not truly mad."

"What do you mean?"

Her stepfather sighed sadly.

"Sometimes we cannot endure the afflictions that the Lord sends to test us."

Richenda considered his answer very carefully. Then she had to admit that she did not understand it. What afflictions had God sent Sir James—beyond the death of his wife? That was a long time ago. Sir James was not ill. Or was he?

"He is defeated, my dear," he urged gently. "Our friend was born to make a flourish in the world. Instead, he is shamed and beggared."

He went on to explain that Sir James had no position of honor for himself; no money for his daughters' dowries; no rents to pay for the repairs to his house.

"He will not even be able to send our beloved Thomas to the university. He is ruined, my dear."

And all this, thought Richenda aghast, was the work of the Lord? She had always been brought up to believe that God had ordained that the Parliament cause should win and that Royalists, such as Sir James, must inevitably suffer defeat. But, suddenly, she was filled with doubts. Had God *really* planned that Thomas should not go to a university—even though He had made him so clever? These were such daring, painful, outrageous thoughts that she kept them to herself.

"And all these misfortunes make Sir James behave as though he is mad?" she asked instead.

Mr. Bemmerton nodded his head. Then he smiled a sad smile.

"He is not so mad, Richenda, that he will not mend—if the times mend."

"What do you mean?"

"If the king should come back to his throne, my child, Sir James will come back to his senses. He will be himself again."

The old man returned to his thoughts, leaving Richenda speechless with surprise.

If the king should come back to his throne . . .

She sat staring at the sixth book of the *Aeneid* with huge, unseeing eyes, wondering if her ears had heard aright. Her stepfather had called Charles Stuart "the king." Her brain seemed to roll over and over like a stone careering down a steep hill. He had called him THE KING. He had spoken as if the times would mend should the king return.

But he was a Puritan! They were all Puritans!

She looked up covertly and gazed at him through her lashes. He was filling the bowl of his pipe with tobacco. He did not look as though he had just said something very startling and strange. Now, he stopped pressing down the tobacco with his finger, sighed, knocked out the contents of the bowl, and lay back in his chair, looking weary and dispirited. As she watched, his brow began knotting up in distress.

He is entering into his grief again, she told herself. There's no help there.

And yet his words—and the thoughts they brought—had somehow to be fitted into her scheme of things.

If the king should come back to his throne . . .

Her father—and Richard's father—had died fighting against the last king. Their fathers' friends had cut off the last king's head. And that—as far as Richenda had been concerned—had been the end of England's ever having kings again. How was it then possible that King Charles II should come back from exile? It seemed an event against God's will—for had not God decreed that the Parliament should win? Had not her father and Richard's father sacrificed their lives to accomplish that decree?

And yet, as she sat there at the study table that late September morning in 1658 and looked at the world that lay beyond the quiet Thames valley, she saw much to disturb her in the state of England. Oliver Cromwell, the lord protector, had died barely three weeks before, and the reins of government had been thrust into the unwilling hands of his son Richard. Her stepfather had shaken his head at the news of the succession. It had seemed to deepen his depression.

"Pray God that chaos is not come again," he declared. "We need wisdom and strength in our rulers, not the timid virtues of poor Richard Cromwell."

In the last few months the outer world had slowly swum into focus in Richenda's mind. And what was now sharp and clear to her view greatly added to her unhappiness. She saw a nation at jangling odds with itself: a people torn by sects and factions; a bitter, disillusioned, violent people—who had lost their joy.

Was it for an England like this that our fathers gave their lives? she wondered sadly. *Is this the only reward for the grief of our parents' wars?*

Sitting there, brooding, she heard a quick intake of breath. She looked up swiftly to see that Mr. Bemmerton's hands were clasped in prayer. Beads of sweat were rolling down his forehead.

"Father, you are ill!" she exclaimed. "Let me call my mother."

The old man opened his eyes and looked at her in a startled manner.

"Ill? . . . Your mother?" he asked.

It was as though he had just come back to her from a long journey.

"You are sweating, father. You are ill."

He passed his hand over his forehead. And then he sighed.

"No, Richenda, I am not ill. Not ill as you think I am ill."

"Then what grieves you so?"

He waited a long time before he replied. Then he spoke quietly.

"I am an old man, my child. In the nature of things, I must soon die."

"Then you *are* ill!" she exclaimed, rising from her chair and coming towards him.

"No, Richenda, I am sick of soul. It is that which ails me."

Greatly disturbed that he should open his grief to her, and yet knowing that for his sake this is what she must hear, she did what she had done as a child. She sat down at his feet and put her head on his knees.

"Tell me," she said gently.

She felt herself tremble. It was the most grown-up thing she had ever said.

"I am filled with grief, my child, at the things I have done in my life that I ought not to have done—and for those many more things that I *should* have done but which I have left undone."

"God will forgive you," she replied.

Mr. Bemmerton let out such a long and wretched sigh that she looked up quickly into his tortured face.

"I pray to God for forgiveness, Richenda," he burst out in anguish. "But I never hear Him say that He has heard me."

Richenda buried her face in the harsh homespun of his breeches—for she was in anguish, too. She also had prayed to the Almighty. Long, long prayers they had been. And the Almighty had never answered her, either.

"But, father," she said at last, putting her own distress behind her. "You are always so good. I cannot believe you have ever done anything sinful."

"You are very young, Richenda."

She lifted up her head and looked at him again.

"Do you think that the young do not understand about sin?" she asked in surprise.

"You do not remember the late wars," he replied, looking down at her and smiling sadly. "That is what I mean."

"What had the wars to do with it?"

Her stepfather's face looked pinched again. He took her hand in his.

"It was terrible time, my dear. A time when father fought against son and brother against brother. A cruel, evil time. No

Christian could live through those years without committing mortal sin."

Richenda looked at the old man in horrified wonder.

"Did you kill someone—when you should not have killed him?" she asked.

He shook his head. But he held her hand in an iron grasp. He had come to the heart of his grief.

"I did not kill," he said bleakly. "But the man's blood is on my soul."

She waited, breathless, for him to explain himself—while the whole adult world of sin and fear and anguish slowly opened up before her astonished eyes.

"I did not know. I did not know," he repeated again and again in his grief. "I thought that Nettlesham was safe . . . that no harm could come to either of you there."

"At Nettlesham? To mother and me?"

"I rode away to London. I left you."

Richenda was greatly puzzled.

"I do not remember Nettlesham," she said.

"I left you both," he repeated starkly.

"But what happened at Nettlesham?" she asked. "Tell me what happened!"

But her stepfather would not tell her. He looked down at her and then seemed to gather himself back into himself. It was as though he had suddenly realized that he was nearly seventy and that she was only fourteen.

"Richenda, dear heart," he concluded gently, taking both her hands in his and bidding her rise. "I thank you for your tenderness. It is a memory of sunshine to me on my dark path. But I have forgotten what a man should never forget."

"What is that?"

"That his soul's grief can be shared with no one—if not with God."

The mystery of what had happened at Nettlesham in the time before she could remember continued to puzzle Richenda during the troubled winter that followed. A man had been killed. But why? How? By whom? And why did her stepfather feel

guilty of his death? Greater wonder of all—what had it to do
with her mother and herself? She could not imagine. No single
story that she could invent would answer all these questions.
The matter remained a mystery.

She watched her mother in the long winter evenings stitching
the hems of her husband's shirts and thought to herself: She
could tell me if I asked her. But Richenda could not ask her.
There was a strange constraint between them.

"Richenda," her mother said one night, "why do you stare at
me so? Are you worried about something?"

"No," she replied quickly, blushing at the lie. "I am not worried about anything."

"Then keep your eyes on your book. It is rude to stare."

At last she told Thomas what her stepfather had let fall.

They were riding through the beech woods. It was February,
and the hills were as quiet as a graveyard.

"Is it not strange?" she asked him. "What can have happened to make him feel so sinful?"

Thomas thought long about the story and then shook his
head.

"I do not know. It is very strange."

"And why should he feel guilty *now*—when it happened so
long ago?"

Thomas thought about this, too.

"Perhaps twelve or thirteen years does not seem so very long
ago when you are as old as Mr. Bemmerton," he suggested.

"And why does he grieve so much that he left us both in
danger?" she wondered. "What kind of danger could it have
been?"

Thomas looked at her and smiled.

"He can acquit himself at least of that—whatever it was,"
he said.

"Why?"

"Because you came safely out of it, Richenda," he laughed.
"You are alive. You are riding beside me now."

Yet, throughout the growing turmoil of that unhappy spring

and summer of 1659, Mr. Bemmerton continued to fret over the future of Richenda and his wife. How could he keep them safe—when he was gone? How, in this tempestuous England of unsettled rule, could he ensure them from all harm? Chaos had indeed come again. Parliament was at odds with the army. And the army was at odds with itself. Wild bands of soldiers swept through the countryside, demanding their pay. The rule of law seemed at an end.

Richenda noticed that her stepfather and mother spent more and more of their time in discussing the management of her Hampshire estate; that they scrimped and saved at Benfield in order to pay off a mortgage on one of her Ropley farms; that tithes and leases and freeholds and the building of barns were the subjects of their fireside talk—not music and the classics, as it used to be.

It is because he thinks he is going to die, she told herself. And he wants to leave things tidy and in order.

No worse an interpretation of his anxious care presented itself to her mind until, one August day, her mother came to sit beside her at the study table. It was a most unusual thing for her to do. It was the middle of the morning.

Richenda pushed aside North's *Plutarch* and turned to her quickly, wondering if her mother were suddenly taken ill.

Yet she looked her quiet and placid self.

"Richenda," she said gently. "It will soon be time for you to leave your studies."

"Why?"

"Because you are growing up, my dear. You must undertake new duties soon."

"New duties? What kind of duties?"

Her mother smiled at her.

"You are fifteen, dear heart. Your stepfather and I must find you a husband."

"A *husband!*" she exclaimed in horror.

What should she do with a husband? A stranger?

"I do not want a husband," she cried out in anguish. "I do not want to marry."

"But, Richenda, all women must marry. It is their duty."

Richenda's whole world seemed to be toppling over a cliff.

"But not now. Not yet," she pleaded desperately. "I am too young to marry."

She could not bear the thought of marriage. It seemed a dungeon to her; a bottomless pit.

Her mother sat beside her, quietly riding the storm.

"I was married at your age, dear child," she said gently. "So was Richard's mother, too."

The nightmare grew worse and worse. She and her stepfather, her mother continued, were already in treaty for a husband for her. There was a family in the North with whom they were in correspondence. Good Puritan gentlefolk. They had a son just suited in age. Nineteen. Reports spoke goldenly of him. He was sober and scholarly. And—what was so fortunate—his father was a large landowner who managed his estates with industry and skill.

"He will teach you both how to administer your father's estates, Richenda."

"But I do not *know* him!" exclaimed Richenda in outrage. "I will not marry someone I do not know!"

She suddenly hated her parents. She felt cornered and trapped.

"Of course you will not," smiled her mother calmly. "That is why we are journeying north next month to stay with the Nortons."

Richenda ran down the lime avenue towards Benfield village, distraught and bitterly enraged. She wanted to escape; to cut herself off; to hide; to go away somewhere quite new. And yet, where could she go? To whom could she turn? It was her own mother—her own stepfather—who were doing her this wrong. People who loved her. People whom she loved. She could not believe it. She could not believe that it was *they* who were preparing her this insult: to marry without knowledge; without love.

"It was not so with my father and yourself when you were young," she had flared at her mother. "I am sure it was not so."

Her mother's quiet reply had shattered all hope.

"My father chose your father for my husband," she said. "We had not met till a fortnight before we were wed."

Then, seeing Richenda's grief, she had taken her in her arms. "My child, my child," she had tried to comfort her. "We were very happy. Very happy in the short time God gave us."

But Richenda was not to be comforted. She suddenly saw that a woman's life was an indignity past all bearing.

She ran on across the fields towards Maplehampden, not thinking where she was going or why, conscious only that the action of running, and the dry scents of the harvest, and the distant flash of the river somehow dulled her clamoring pain. She was going back . . . back . . . back. But where? Where was there to go back to? Childhood was over. There was no comfort there. Yet, as she ran on past the foot of Hampden Hill, she began to feel strangely numbed and disembodied, as though she were not the Richenda who was so soon to be married, but the true, essential Richenda: the Richenda whom nobody knew about except herself.

"They cannot *make* me marry," she gulped angrily. "They cannot. No. They cannot."

When she came to the Maplehampden mill, her whole past was waiting there to confront her. Thomas. Richard. Her mother. Her stepfather. They were the four pillars of her world. And her mother and her stepfather wanted her to marry. To marry a man called Francis. Francis Norton. Someone she had never even heard of four hours ago.

She tore open the tumbledown door of the disused mill, climbed up into the loft, and flung herself down on a heap of chaff.

"Oh, God," she wept. "Why do I love them so much? Why can't I hate them instead?"

Exhausted at last by her grief and by running so far, she dropped into a fitful, unhappy doze, from which she awakened a few minutes later to a fresh understanding of her plight and a fresh storm of tears. Was it for this that her mother had loved her? Was it for this that her stepfather had taught her so carefully—as if she had been his own son? What had happened?

Why had they stopped treating her as herself? Why was she now only a property to be disposed of with prudence?

"I am my father's estate," she wept bitterly. "I am my father's estate that needs a skillful manager. I am not a girl. Not Richenda any more."

So it went on all that long August day. She wept and then slept. Then, woke again—and wept again.

When the sun had sunk to the west and the light was pouring slantwise through the wide cracks in the shuttered window, she heard faint shouts coming from the Maplehampden lawns. And then, almost immediately, there was a gentle scraping of feet on the rungs of the ladder below.

Someone was coming up into the loft.

"Thomas!" she exclaimed in surprise, as his head emerged through the square in the floor.

She had not known that Thomas had come home from school.

"Richenda," he whispered, in concern as he looked searchingly at her tear-stained face.

Their eyes were on the same level, his as he came up through the floor and hers as she lay on the heap of chaff.

"Richenda, what has happened? They are anxious. They are looking for you."

Richenda burst into a fresh storm of tears—for a new and overwhelming grief had now overtaken her. She had seen Thomas's strained, tender, anxious face in the barred shafts of light. It was *Thomas*. It was Thomas they were taking her away from. Of course it was Thomas. Why had she not understood it before? She buried her face in her hands.

He was kneeling now beside her amongst the chaff.

"Richenda," he whispered. "Don't cry. Don't cry. They will hear you. But tell me—please tell me what has happened."

She told him in gulps the sorry tale—drearily almost—her lips moving, but with the spirit gone out of her rage, while all the time her eyes, unbidden, noticed the frays in his cuffs and the way his arms had grown too long for his shirt. He listened, holding her head against his shoulder, as they had done as children when they were sad. And, when she had come to an end, he sat there in an unhappy, compassionate silence, refusing to comfort her with easy, empty words.

"Perhaps it is God's will," he sighed at last in wretchedness. "No, it is *not*," Richenda almost shouted, jumping to her feet. "It is *not* God's will."

He looked up, startled, into her proud, angry, insulted face.

"God has not put it into my heart that I should marry yet," she declared.

Thomas leaped up from the floor and clutched both her hands.

"Richenda," he said excitedly, forcing her to look him in the eyes. "Does this mean God talks to you? Does it? Does it? Did God really tell you that you should not marry this man?"

Richenda returned his gaze and suddenly felt utterly broken. She could deceive herself. She could not deceive Thomas. Ever.

"God has not said a word," she whispered, engulfed in misery. "He has never said a word to me all my life long."

She bowed her head. It seemed to her the final admission of the failure that had darkened the last twelve months. She had lost her faith. She was cast out adrift in a huge, uncaring universe. There was no wise Father in Heaven whose special care she was.

Thomas could not have followed her into the depths of her despair, for he was talking very quickly and excitedly, the words tumbling over each other just as they had done when he was a child.

"It is because we are always talking to Him, Richenda, and never giving ourselves time to listen to His reply. That is what it is. I am sure it is. In our Anglican Church we speak to Him in the most beautiful English. You would not know—but they are the most beautiful prayers we say at home when the priest comes. Beautiful. But we never listen to what *He* has to say to *us*. And it is the same with you Puritans. I know from going to the church at Wittendon. The minister prays to God in a long kind of bullying harangue. And then he stands up in the pulpit and tells us all about the pains of Hell."

His words whirred like fireflies round the darkening loft. Richenda heard them; but they did not enter her mind. She was noting instead that he looked thin and overgrown and strung tight—like her lute. Yet that he was strong, somehow, in a way that neither Richard nor herself was strong; that he had hope and courage and that he had retained his faith.

She knew then that she loved him. A great tenderness for him swept over her—a tenderness that gave her strength to face what had to be faced.

"God has not told me what to do, Thomas," she said calmly. "So I will go with them, into Furness, to the Nortons as they bid."

He looked at her in sudden pain.

"But I will not marry Francis. I shall *never* marry him."

5
✵ Richard Disgraces Himself

NEWS of the Bemmertons' intended journey north—
and the reason for it—reached Richard towards the end of his
first month as an undergraduate at Oxford.

"Seeing the tangle of the times, they wish to see Richenda
wed," Thomas wrote bleakly.

Richard dropped his letter to the floor and stared out of his
attic window at the steep roof-tops and the turrets and the
spires gleaming in the rain, utterly cast down with wretchedness.

Had it come so soon? So very soon? She was barely fifteen!

He had not seen Richenda since Christmas, for his stepfather
had kept him at his side during the following two holidays,
making him study hard for his entry to the university. He had
thought Richard lazy and stupid and too much given over to
foolish experiments in natural philosophy.

"You have your way to make in the world, young man," Mr.
Drew had rasped. "You must put away childish things now."

And so Richard had not seen Richenda for nine months. In
the long, empty weeks of his absence she had become more an
idea to him than a person—a flash of fair hair, a smile, a
strong, defiant, moody girl: someone so vital and full of beauty

that he caught his breath whenever he thought of her. And yet, somehow, he did not feel he *knew* this vision. Ever since that day by the weir at Maplehampden, Richenda had continually surprised him. Her nature always seemed to be changing; even her looks altered. She was like a face beckoning to him out of the surface of a lake.

And now she was to be married off against her will, Thomas wrote. Richenda was to be forced into wedlock with a man that not one of them knew. His heart dropped like a stone.

Then he grew angry. Why were the Bemmertons hurrying Richenda away? Why had they been so certain that they must seek a husband for her elsewhere than at home? For pity's sake, why had they not given Thomas and himself more time— time to grow to be men? He sat there miserably with his Greek text spread out in front of him, staring out at the sheets of rain blown sideways across the sky and at the runnels of water spouting out of the gargoyles, and condemned the Bemmertons most bitterly for betraying the three of them.

It was a grievous time for him, that autumn and winter of 1659. Everything was going wrong.

He had come up to Oxford eager, indeed, to throw off "childish things." He had wanted to be a man. He had also wanted to study mathematics, to experiment in chemistry, and to hear those new truths expounded that Dr. Boteler had described so glowingly in the long correspondence that they had had. Instead, he found himself bound in thrall to Obadiah Drew—his stepfather's son by his first marriage—a narrow scholar and a canting rogue, who beat him hard into his Latin and Greek and even harder into a stupid pedantry that Richard neither wished to know nor, indeed, could understand.

"You are even more stupid and stubborn than my father said," Obadiah told him one day, throwing down his rod and wiping his clammy face.

And Richard, who had endured the rod at school because he had feared to go begging for his bread, began to wonder whether a life on the road were really the worst fortune that could befall a man. That he should have ever been assigned to

such a tutor seemed to him the most cruel piece of injustice that
had yet come his way. He saw now that his stepfather had a
sour streak of fair dealing in his nature. He had sent him to
school and kept him in meat and clothing for seven years of his
life. And he was now sending him to the university. But his son
Obadiah had not a hair-breadth of honesty in his soul. He was
a cruel, hypocritical, pious bigot.

In his misery, Richard behaved like a fool. He was so em-
bittered by the Bemmertons, so enraged by Obadiah, and so disappointed in his hopes of taking part in scientific experiments,
that he assumed a wildness and conceit that made him despicable to the two or three kindly scholars to whom Dr. Boteler had
furnished him with an introduction. Warden Wilkins of Wadham College, for example—a most noted experimentalist in the
New Science—had greeted him affably and had set a young gentleman commoner of his college to teach Richard his Euclid,
but, noting his boastful manner, had failed to invite him to one
of his philosophical evenings and had never inquired after him
further. Richard was greatly cast down in his own esteem. The
Bemmertons had failed him. Oxford had failed him. And he
had failed himself.

So he took to entertaining Bob Reeves and Jack Scudamore
at the alehouse and to tarts and comfits in his room. And when
his stepfather's meager allowance had come to an end—since
Bob had a viol and Jack a pipe and himself the fine lute that
Mrs. Bemmerton had given him—the three of them dressed up
as mummers and walked out into the country and played on the
village greens. The country people gave them bread at Hampton Poyle, ale at Bletchingdon, and a few groats at Weston-on-
the-Green.

Obadiah soon heard of their frolics, beat Richard hard, and
wrote home to tell his father how badly his pupil had behaved.
And then Richard was given not a penny piece of his own. His
friends took themselves off to richer game. And he was left to
spend his days wretchedly—when he was not cracking his brains
over logic—gazing into the booksellers' shops at the maps and
globes that he could never buy, and envying other men their

powdered hair, their laced bands and tassels, and their Spanish leather boots.

It was a bad time in England's history to have been caught in —just when one was floundering from a boy into a man. The country had drifted into a prolonged state of crisis. Parliament was divided and powerless; fanatics prophesied doom. It was a bad time to be up at Oxford, too, for the discord of the times jangled even louder in the city's narrow lanes and courts than elsewhere in the realm. The turmoil excited Richard; it excited his friends. After the boredom of schooldays, this was life.

They plotted and drank toasts in the alehouses and came out into the streets and shouted for—they knew not what.

Then, General Monck and his army began marching south from Scotland. And Richard, together with thousands upon thousands of other young Englishmen, turned his eyes and his heart northwards to watch the general's slow, deliberate approach. For in Monck they saw a savior from the great disorders of the day. Monck, surely, would call a free Parliament. Monck, surely, would restrain the pillaging of the armies. Monck would restore dignity and honor to a troubled land.

"A free Parliament! A free Parliament!" shouted the undergraduates of Oxford.

"Monck and a free Parliament!" shouted Richard.

Obadiah and his logic could go hang. This was no time to be a pedant.

And then, in that January of 1660, an Anabaptist preacher in St. Peters-in-the-Bailey denounced the students' clamor and threatened them with eternal damnation for their pains. And— wonder of all wonders—the vice-chancellor stopped this same preacher and had him thrown out of the church. Men began to speak guardedly behind their hands of King Charles II coming to his own again. And one bitter night, very early in February, Jack Scudamore and Richard—on a dare from Bob Reeves— climbed out of their college, stole a builder's ladder and a chisel, and chipped away the plaster that for the last ten years had covered up the royal coat of arms over the college gate, so that the rampant lion stood white and blinking to the world when the morning came. Obadiah, suspecting his part in this prank, grew more spiteful and savage each time Richard came to him. He roared at him, calling him a rogue and a traitor to the true religion, promising him beggary in this world and damnation in the next if he did not mend his ways. And Richard, flushed with the growing hope of the times, saw clearly that a free Parliament and the return of the king might mean the end of Obadiah's cruel power over him, and—like a fool—answered him wildly and with impudence.

And then, on the night of February 13, news reached them at Oxford of General Monck's declaration for a free Parliament.

The whole city went mad. The church bells rang. Bonfires were lit in the street. And the undergraduates took to the taverns and drank a health to Monck, and another to the new Parliament, and another to the king, and yet another to their great country of England. Richard and his contemporaries, who had all been born in the dismal years, had never known such a lightening of men's hearts.

Reeling out of the tavern in Blue Boar Lane, he came out into High Street, and saw a gathering outside the gate of All Souls, and smelled a savory smell.

"What do they do?" he asked a citizen coming away.

The citizen laughed.

"Burning the old Rump Parliament."

"How so?"

"Why, by burning rumps of beef," he said.

Richard pressed into the crowd and saw the blackening rumps sizzling on a pit hung across a great fire of coals. And, as he watched, a man pulled off a rump, laughing savagely, and heaved it up through a window into All Souls.

"Ah!" sighed the crowd, suddenly quiet with satisfaction.

And then, as the glass broke, they yelled and laughed and jeered like the devils in Hell.

"Whose window is that?" he asked.

"Dr. John Palmer's," cried another undergraduate. "And a pox on all the rest of Oliver Cromwell's friends."

Now Richard, being three-quarters drunk and seeing an ox's liver that someone had thrust on the spit beside the rumps, snatched at the liver and carried it, burning and sticky in his hands, as he ran up Catte Street. And when he had come to Broad Street he stood below Obadiah's window and shouted a great shout.

"And the same to all such lying Presbyterian knaves as you, Obadiah Drew."

And he threw the charred liver straight into the clammy face of his astonished tutor, who had come to the window to see who had called.

What a folly is drunkenness!

He ruined himself that stupid night. For Obadiah, seeing him

laughing at him in the street below, came roaring down the
stairs, waving his rod, and began belaboring him over the head.
But Richard, elated by drinking so many toasts, was no longer a
boy in his own esteem. He was no longer a child to be whipped.
He was a man. He snatched at his tutor's rod and threw it high
over the roof of Trinity. Then he turned, clenched his fist, and

hit his half-brother hard on the bridge of his busy, sin-prying, fanatical nose.

"I've done with you," he shouted exultantly, leaving him gasping on the ground.

But, alas, it was not Richard who had done with Obadiah; it was Richard's whole family who had done with him!

Four days later a terrible letter arrived from his stepfather. He disowned him, he wrote. From now onwards Richard was denied his home, his purse, and the use of his influence. Mr. Drew would do nothing more for him. He had sent him to school; he had paid his fees at the university; and he would have given him his support in following a legal career. And how had Richard repaid his kindness? With insult. With the grossest insult. His violent and ungoverned behavior to his half-brother had forfeited him all rights to his stepfather's protection. He sent Richard a small sum of money to pay his debts and bade him take his few belongings and be gone from Oxford immediately, for he no longer wished to be shamed by so infamous a stepson in such a grave and learned place. Richard was forbidden to write to him or ever attempt to see him again.

Richard's mother wrote more bitterly still.

She said that he had disgraced his father's name and that he had mocked the cause for which his father had given his life. She no longer recognized him as her son, she wrote.

"Your birth was a grief to me," she added. "Your childhood a heavy burden, and now in your young manhood you have broken my heart. I never wish to see you or to hear your name again."

Richard was appalled.

His stepfather's anger was just, he saw. And his mother's harsh farewell was perhaps no more than he should have expected.

But that he had mocked his father's death! This gave him the sharpest pain he had yet known.

His father was his father. He loved him. His pride in his father was the most precious thing he had.

He was wretched. He felt utterly adrift. He wanted to pack

up his few books, sling his lute across his back, and run straight off to Benfield. He wanted to be with Richenda. With Thomas. He wanted them to tell him that he had not mocked his father. Or—if he had mocked him—that his father, watching him from heaven, had forgiven him his folly. For folly it was, indeed. He saw now very clearly that King Charles II meant nothing to him. He knew nothing about politics. As long as England was at peace and prosperous—and he, Richard, was free of the hateful Obadiah—he cared not who ruled the realm. In his anguish he wanted his two friends desperately.

But Thomas had not written to him for months. Richenda and the Bemmertons must still be away in the North, he thought. And what comfort was there in Richenda—wherever she was? She was married to a stranger. She was cut off from him now forever.

And Thomas?

Richard was ashamed to go to Thomas. Thomas had so longed to go to Oxford with him, and he, Richard, had made such a clownish use of his time there that he had not the courage to tell his friend how he had been sent away. He had wasted his chances. He had been an utter fool. He had, somehow, let Thomas down. He could not bear to tell him what had happened.

And so, humbled and lonely and feeling deeply ashamed, he shouldered his pack and set out for London. He was going to walk to Wood Street, off Cheapside. To Dr. Phineas Boteler.

"Pray God the old man will overlook my folly," he thought, "and offer to pick me up out of the gutter."

6
❀ In the North

FOUR months earlier Richenda and her parents had driven north in the clumsy old coach—an unhappy family, grievously at odds with itself.

"We want your happiness, only that, Richenda," her mother said sharply, frowning at her daughter's rebellious face.

"Am I not to be a judge of what makes me happy?" Richenda burst out. "Is it not *my* life you are ordering?"

"You must trust us, dear child," said Mr. Bemmerton gently. "We are older than you. We know the world's sad ways."

Heartsick, all three of them were skirmishing in the age-old battle of the generations.

Deep down, Richenda felt as calm as the bottom of the sea. She loved Thomas. She would never marry anyone except Thomas. But on the surface all sorts of contrary winds were blowing. She was at war with her parents; they were at war with her. She was not used to fighting them; and she felt angry and hurt and more than a little frightened at the blustery storm brewing inside the jolting coach.

"Why, then, have you kept me in ignorance of the world?" she asked her stepfather bitterly.

They had brought her up almost in solitude at Benfield. They

78

had never been to London since the days of her infancy. They had never visited kinsmen. She had known no one save Richard and Thomas. Why had they not taken her out and shown her the "world's sad ways"?

"But, Richenda," expostulated her mother, "you are only a girl."

"Have we not done right, dear heart, to protect you from knowing what is harmful?" said Mr. Bemmerton.

No, they had not done right. They had done a great wrong.

"You treat me like a plaything," Richenda sobbed angrily. "Something to be kept in ignorance and protected. And then . . . then . . . when you grow old . . . and you think you are going to die . . . you . . . you . . . have to find someone . . . for me in a hurry. A man . . . a stranger . . . to hand me over to . . ."

"Richenda!" exclaimed her mother, appalled at the bitterness in her voice. "You are speaking of your parents—your *parents*. We love you!"

Was it love to have educated her as a boy? Was it love to have taught her to think for herself? Was it love to have snatched her away from Thomas?

"Then, if you love me," she said, turning upon them fiercely, "give me leave to choose my husband for myself."

Having so unexpectedly heaved her heart into her mouth, she waited, aghast, for their answer.

"But, my child," said Mrs. Bemmerton in astonishment, "seeing we have lived so retired a life, you do not know a man suitable to be your husband!"

Richenda stared at her mother in blank amazement.

"You know no one but Richard and Thomas," she continued. "And they are only boys."

Stunned by her words, she continued to stare at her mother, unable at first to believe that she could be so blind. Then, as the truth dawned on her, Richenda wanted to shout aloud in outrage: "We are the same age. If Thomas is too young to be a husband, then I am too young to be a wife." But she did nothing of the kind. She bit her lip, withdrew into her corner of the coach, and stared out at the sleeting rain. Thomas was too precious to be bandied about between them. Besides, the true nature of her affection for him was too new and too secret—even to herself. She did not know whether Thomas returned her love. And it was all too surprising and dazzling. It was like the brilliance of the summer sun. One could look at it only in short blinks.

Mr. Bemmerton had sunk into one of his brooding fits. He looked so harrowed with tortured thought—and had looked thus harrowed so often in the past twelve months—that Richenda had almost forgotten the happy old man of her childhood. She had only added to his grief, she thought with compunction.

"Perhaps Richenda is right, Susannah," he said at last. "Perhaps we should have shown her more of the world before we arranged her marriage."

Her mother waited in silence for him to continue. It was her strength, Richenda thought, that she never contradicted her husband.

Her stepfather went on to suggest that they should break their journey at Burford and drive on to Shipton-under-Wychwood to visit his kinsman there.

"He has a family of young people," he explained. "And they will be able to show Richenda—and ourselves, too, my dear—how it is with girls in this modern age."

The visit brought none of them much relief. The kinsman was as harassed by the disorders of the times as Mr. Bemmerton. He had married one daughter advantageously to a London merchant twice her age. She wrote happily, he said, and continually expressed gratitude that her father had arranged so wealthy a match for her. Her husband had just been made an alderman, she wrote, and they had ordered a carriage from the coachmaker. But he had failed to marry off his younger daughter. Times were bad, he said. The harvest had been ruined by the great storms at the beginning of September, and he could not afford a dowry commensurate with the one he had given his elder girl.

"She will have to bide her time," he told Mr. Bemmerton grimly, "till there is a rise in the price of wheat."

Yet it was not the fate of the sulky daughter left husbandless at home that affected Richenda so much. It was the quiet misery of Charity—a girl of her own age—married to the kinsman's eldest son. Charity was her mother-in-law's butt and slave. It was "Charity, do this"—"Charity, do that"—"Charity, sit up straight"—"Charity, in this family we *never* open a book before noon." Richenda looked into the girl's bewildered, unhappy eyes and thought that her heart would break were she in Charity's place. It came to her with a shudder that were she to marry Francis Norton, *his* mother might treat *her* thus! These were the world's sad ways! She clutched at the memory of Thomas. Thomas was her talisman. He gave her courage.

Charity's predicament had not escaped the Bemmertons, either. And, to tell the truth, they had both been sickened by their kinsman's hard-headed bartering of daughters. They were unworldly; they wished only for Richenda's happiness and safety.

Two days later they resumed their journey north towards Worcester, all three of them sunk even deeper in gloom.

It was a terrible journey that they had that stormy autumn, for not only were the drovers' roads made impassable by the heavy rains, so that they had to travel miles out of their way, seeking higher ground above the great lakes of mud, but they had also to wait for days on end at wayside inns and at coach stages for baggage trains and outriders to accompany them over heaths and commons, for it was no time for an old man, a woman, and a girl to be journeying abroad, unprotected and alone. Disbanded, penniless soldiers roamed the fields, holding up travellers and demanding that they should render them their long arrears in pay, while thieves and highwaymen, emboldened by the disorders of the times, infested the more desolate stretches of the main roads. Men sought safety in numbers and travelled in convoy, or not at all.

They did not reach Lancaster until the middle of November, and, by this time, Mr. Bemmerton was so exhausted by the cold and by the continual jolting of the old coach over the ruts and holes in the way—and made so miserable by his inward grief—that he was utterly spent. Richenda's mother looked at her husband and insisted that they should stay at the best inn which the place could provide so that he might recoup his strength.

Richenda watched him stagger wearily and in pain up to his inn bedroom and was overcome with remorse.

"He has undertaken this terrible journey for my sake," she thought, conscience-stricken. "And it is all useless. Quite useless. We ought never to have come."

When she carried him up his supper that night and saw that he was too exhausted even to eat, she felt torn by her feelings of guilt. She sat by the bedroom fire and watched the soft light from the coals playing over his worn features and closed, sunken eyes.

"Why cannot I tell him about Thomas?" she thought unhappily. "Why cannot I confess to him that I shall never marry the man he has chosen for me?"

Later, when he had fallen into an uneasy sleep, and her mother had gone down to the ostler to inquire about the horses, she stood by his bed and looked down on his pale countenance, noticing the blue lines under his eyes and on either side of the bridge of his nose.

"What if he should die?" she asked herself in anguish. "What if this fearful journey should cause his death?"

But Mr. Bemmerton did not die. All he needed was rest and warmth and their tender care, which they gave him without

stint—and an ease from his soul's torment, which they could not give. Seeing him grow stronger in body but still cast down in his thoughts, Richenda wondered to herself:

"What strange sin can it be that still haunts him so?"

It was like a canker; it was turning him into someone quite unlike himself. Her mother, too, was becoming infected by his gloom and, seeking its cause, found it in Richenda's wilful refusal to think of marriage.

"See how you are distressing your stepfather, Richenda!" she exclaimed sharply one morning. "He would be happy if only you would trust us to know what is best."

But she refused to trust her parents. She told them so.

They set off northwards again at the beginning of December in bright, frosty weather and drove along the shore of Morecambe Bay to Silverdale. Richenda gazed out over the bay, her heart ready to burst into flower at the beauty of the scene. The tide was going out. The freshness and smoothness of the great stretches of silver-gold sand which the receding sea uncovered awoke feelings of joy inside her which she had almost forgotten.

"That is the way we are going, my child," smiled Mr. Bemmerton, seeing the beauty of the sands reflected in her face.

"The way? What do you mean?"

"Across the sands."

Mr. Bemmerton pointed across the bay to the low hills rising above Grange and explained that they would bait the horses at Silverdale, wait for the tide to ebb further, and then gallop across the three miles of sand to the farther shore of the bay. It saved twenty miles and more by the road.

"We must gallop as fast as we can," he smiled, "or else we shall be caught by the incoming tide."

Richenda was still enough of a child to be excited. And, half an hour later, as they flew over the sparkling sands, the horses' hoofs throwing up little flying crumbles of silver-gold and the wheels of the coach leaving their lonely tracks behind them, she felt momentarily carried back into a world of enchantment.

But she was a girl, too: a girl who was being driven into Furness to meet a husband.

She looked at the farther shore growing closer and more distinct with every fresh lunge of the galloping horses and realized
that the supreme moment of crisis was almost upon her. Beyond
that hill and the next—and across another stretch of sand—
they would come into Furness, to Ulverston. And at Ulverston
she would have to confront her mother and her stepfather and
the Nortons with her final refusal.

She glanced quickly at the two of them, sitting beside her.

"When we come back across these sands," she thought with
an ache throbbing in her throat, "they will hate me."

Next day they arrived at the Nortons' house. And the final
stages of the match-making were begun in earnest.

"Francis," bellowed Mr. Norton in good-natured raillery.
"Look up, boy! You'll not see Richenda in the carpet. Look up
and use your eyes!"

Richenda was covered with confusion. She knew that she was
scarlet in the face. So was Francis. He could not bear to raise
his eyes to hers.

"Give them time, dear friend," murmured her stepfather.

"Take Richenda into the long gallery, Francis," suggested
his mother.

"Young people feel awkward in front of their parents,"
Richenda heard her mother telling the Nortons as the two of
them left the room.

Up in the long gallery, Francis was even more confused. He
did not know what to do or say. He left her standing in the
middle of the floor and strode off to the far end by the pictures,
and then, thinking no doubt that he was being grossly uncivil,
he strode back again towards her and stood in front of her, his
hands hanging limply at his side.

She looked at him with compassion. He was tall and thin and
had a slight stoop.

"Francis," she said gently. "Look at me. Don't be afraid."

Unwillingly, he raised his eyes to hers, and she looked into a
gentle soul, goaded almost beyond bearing.

"I am only a girl," she said, smiling a little uncertainly. "I
think I feel as frightened as you do."

His eyes now looked as though they were really seeing her. He scanned her narrowly as though she were a book, his gaze coming to rest at last on her own eyes.

"Do you want to marry me, Richenda?" he gulped. His voice sounded sick with fear.

"No," she replied simply.

A cloud seemed to lift momentarily from him. Then he sighed. The cloud had settled back down again.

"Do *you* want to marry *me?*" she asked him.

He shook his head. He seemed bowed in shame.

There was no shame in Richenda. She felt like a rocket bursting into stars. He did not want to marry her! He did not want to marry her! She felt intoxicated by joy. She wanted to throw her arms round him in pure friendship. Instead, she took him gently by the hand and led him towards the door.

"We must tell our parents," she said.

He tore himself from her grasp.

"We cannot," he cried out in despair. "My father has ordained that we should marry. It is suitable, he says . . ."

Richenda turned on him in a fury.

"Francis, it is *our* lives they are ordaining—not their own. I will not marry you. I shall never consent to marry you."

Francis looked at her in astonished disbelief.

"But you do not know my father . . ." he began.

She stamped her foot.

"Do not be such a coward," she stormed.

Then, seeing that she was only frightening him when she wanted to give him courage, she took him to the window-seat and told him quietly, but sternly, what the two of them must do. They must tell their parents. They must ride the storm. They must be steadfast. They must be brave. They must give each other courage.

"They will be very angry," he warned her.

"Yes, and it will be worse than that," she said. "Our mothers will weep and say that we do not love them. They will reproach us for months and months."

"I think my father will beat me and turn me out of his house," said Francis.

Richenda looked at him aghast.

"*Beat* you—for not marrying me?"

He nodded his head and turned away.

"But Francis, he cannot do that!" she exclaimed. "Not if it is *I* who refuse to marry *you!*"

"And your father? Will he not beat you if you say such a thing?" he asked.

She shook her head. He had never beaten her, she said.

Then she smiled, a new thought coming into her head.

"He cannot even be very angry with me," she said, smiling broadly, "if it is *you* who refuse to marry *me!*"

If they were both equally determined, she declared, they were invincible.

The Nortons bullied Francis and Richenda for three terrible, nerve-racking days. Mr. Norton stormed and Mrs. Norton wept. At length, the Bemmertons—more clearly aware of Richenda's determination than the Nortons were of their son's—took their leave, saddened and humiliated. With a quietly triumphant daughter sitting between them, they took to the road again on their long journey home.

Their uneasiness with each other and their embarrassment at the farce in which they had all played a part, seemed hardly the mood in which, suddenly—like Saul on the road to Damascus—to enter a new spiritual life.

Yet, so it was.

In a wayside inn, not two miles from Ulverston, they were to experience the most important event of their lives.

The old coach was lumbering through a dirty village of miserable shacks, when two girls on horseback unexpectedly galloped out from a side road. Their appearance startled Mr. Bemmerton's sturdy nags, who reared up on their hind legs and then bolted. The coach swung this way and that between the scattered hovels and then overturned against a tree.

Richenda found herself sprawling in a ditch on top of her mother.

"Are you all right, mother?" she cried, scrambling quickly to her feet. "Oh, please God you are not hurt!"

Mrs. Bemmerton blinked up at her and then smiled.

"Help me up, child. I am not hurt. But how is your father? Where is he?"

They found Mr. Bemmerton pinned by the foot under the wheel of the upturned coach.

"Father, cried Richenda, flinging herself down on her knees beside him.

"Isaac. Dear Isaac," cried her mother.

"All is well, dear hearts," he reassured them with a smile. "Except for my ankle. I cannot move it."

The two girls had ridden up by this time, had dismounted in haste, and were running towards them.

"Dear sir," cried the elder one, "it was our fault. It was all our fault."

"Sarah," cried the younger girl, "help me to lift the wheel from his leg."

Richenda looked at her in surprise. She was barely more than a child. She looked about twelve.

"We will all try," said Mrs. Bemmerton, suiting the action to the word.

The four of them—Richenda and her mother and Sarah and the child—strained and heaved at the wheel of the heavy coach. But it was too much for them.

A number of women from the village had now gathered in a small crowd about them.

"Is there no man can save you this heavy task?" asked Mr. Bemmerton patiently.

"Mary," panted the elder girl, "mount your pony and ride quickly to John Drinkall at the smithy. John will help us. And then ride on to Swarthmoor. Tell mother that we have caused an accident."

Ten minutes later John Drinkall, with the help of the remaining three of them, had freed Mr. Bemmerton from the wheel; but as they lifted the rim off his leg they saw that his ankle was cut and twisted. They stood and looked at it in consternation.

"Like as not, friend, the ankle be broke," rumbled the burly blacksmith.

"What shall we do?" Mrs. Bemmerton asked her husband. "Were it not best that we send word to the Nortons?"

"No!" exclaimed Richenda and her stepfather together.

"Then I'll carry you to the inn, friend," said the blacksmith.

"No! No!" interrupted Sarah, "Mother will want to care for you at home. You cannot go to the inn."

"But, my child," expostulated Mr. Bemmerton weakly, "we are strangers. We cannot trespass upon your mother's time."

"You are mistaken, friend," said the blacksmith. "No one in trouble in Furness is a stranger to Margaret Fell."

Richenda looked down at her stepfather, awaiting his reply.

"He has fainted," she cried. "Look, my father has fainted."

His eyes fluttered open again and he smiled fleetingly.

It was bitterly cold for him, lying there on the ground. An

east wind was blowing across the wide estuary stretched out below them.

"Please carry my husband to the inn," Mrs. Bemmerton said, turning to John Drinkall. "He is ill. And it is cold. We cannot leave him here."

Half an hour later they had the old man lying flat on a table in an upstairs room. The beds and the bedding were damp, Mrs. Bemmerton had declared, and it was better to have him thus, wrapped up in their own cloaks and rugs. The woman of the house had been surly; but she had lit them a small fire of coals.

Sarah was almost in tears.

"I cannot forgive myself that we should have caused you such harm," she said wretchedly.

"But it was an accident," replied Richenda. "One cannot help these things."

She looked at Sarah Fell anew and saw a fine, well-grown girl a little older than herself. She was clearly a gentlewoman, but there was nothing affected or womanish about her; she was dressed sensibly and well; but there were no frills. She was full of strength and vigor. Yet she was sensitive, too. And honest. She had bravely shouldered responsibility for what had happened.

"I like her," Richenda told herself. "I like everything about her. And I like the blacksmith, too."

There was a clatter of horses' hoofs by the inn door, and Sarah ran to the bedroom window, peered down, and cried:

"It is mother! Thanks be to the Lord! All now will be well."

Mr. Bemmerton proved too ill to be carried to Swarthmoor Hall, even had he so wished it, for the shock and the pain of the accident and the intense cold, together with the great mental discomfort of their visit to the Nortons, had brought on a fever. He wandered in his mind all that evening and the succeeding day. And when he came to himself at nightfall he was weak and greatly cast down, having fallen back again into the old torment of his former grief.

Mrs. Fell visited them three times those first twenty-four

hours, bringing dry mattresses, blankets, clean linen—and broth
and apples and a great Swarthmoor meat pie. Yet her chief concern was not for her patient's body, but for his spirit.

"Isaac is not dangerously ill in his flesh, Susannah," she told
Richenda's mother. "His ankle is not broken; and his fever will
pass. It is his spirit that is in travail."

Mrs. Bemmerton nodded her head. She knew this, too.

"Wilt thou give me leave, Susannah, to sit with Isaac and
pray with him?"

Richenda watched her mother look up, perplexed and irreso-
lute. Neither of them was used to people calling them by their
Christian names upon so slight an acquaintance. Nor were they
used to strangers praying alone with those they held dear.

"Sometimes a soul in trouble will open to a stranger," Margaret Fell explained. "Indeed, it has been often thus."

And so it came about that the plump, sturdy, middle-aged
owner of Swarthmoor Hall rode over the moor early and late,
climbed the narrow stairs to the cramped inn bedroom, and sat
with Mr. Bemmerton, reading and praying, while Richenda and
her mother sat in the room below, gazing out at the desolate
Furness landscape, constrained with each other because of Francis Norton, and both puzzled by the strange frankness and loving concern of their new acquaintance.

"What can they be doing?" Mrs. Bemmerton asked her
daughter, as she strained her ears for the sound of voices coming through the ceiling. "They have not said a word for the last
half-hour!"

Of what nature was her stepfather's terrible sin? wondered
Richenda. And why were they sitting so long in silence?

"We were waiting upon the Lord, dear hearts," he told them
that night. "We were emptying our minds of worldly things.
We were sweeping clean a room to entertain the Lord."

"You sat here and said nothing?" asked Richenda's mother
doubtfully. "You did not even pray?"

"Why, yes, Susannah, of course we prayed. But we sat in silence afterwards, listening for His answer."

Richenda pricked up her ears. It reminded her of something

that Thomas had once said. Yes. Thomas. In the loft. When she had cried so much.

"And did He answer you?" she asked eagerly.

Her stepfather raised his arms to them both. His face was flushed with hope.

"Dear hearts, a light is dawning for me out of my darkness."

He made them sit beside him, and he then handed his wife a piece of paper on which there was much writing.

"Read this, dear Susannah. Margaret brought it to me. It has given me much comfort."

Richenda watched her mother read the paper, her brows creasing up as she struggled to decipher the cramped writing. But it seemed to bring her mother comfort, too—despite her difficulty in reading it.

"Who wrote it?" she asked softly, laying it down at her side.

"It is a copy of a letter written by George Fox."

"Who is he?"

"A letter to Mrs. Fell?" Richenda asked.

"No. To Lady Claypole."

"To Lady Claypole!" exclaimed her mother. "The Lord Protector's daughter?"

Her stepfather nodded his head.

"She was dying of cancer and she was much troubled by the remembrance of her sins. George Fox wrote to her thus. And it brought her great solace."

"May I read the letter, too?" Richenda asked shyly.

"Give it to her, Susannah."

And Richenda, taking the close writing to the light of the window, read as follows:

Friend—Be still and cool in thy own mind and spirit from thy own thoughts and then thou wilt feel the principle of God to turn thy mind to the Lord. . . . That is it which works up into patience, innocency . . . into stillness, . . . quietness up to God.

This then is the word of the Lord God unto you all; whatever temptations, distractions, confusions, the light [of God] doth make manifest and discover, do not look at these temptations, confusions, corruptions; but look at the light, which discovers them and makes them manifest, and with the same light you may feel over them, to receive power to withstand them. The same light which lets you see sin and transgression, will let you see the covenant of God, which blots out your sin and transgression. For looking down at sin . . . ye are swallowed up in it; but looking at the light, which discovers them, ye will see over them. That will give victory; and ye will find grace and strength; there is the first step to peace. . . .

G.F.

When she had finished reading the letter she turned back to the room and looked at her stepfather's face, transformed, as it now was, by a living hope.

"My dears," he said to them both. "I think I have just stumbled upon that first step to peace."

He told them that he wanted to learn much more about this strange sect of Margaret Fell's and that if he had recovered his strength sufficiently and the coach were repaired in time they should all attend a meeting of the sect at Swarthmoor Hall on Sunday.

"On Sunday! But that is only three days' time!" exclaimed his wife. "You cannot be well enough by then!"

"The Lord is a mighty healer, Susannah," he replied with a smile, "when a man has a mind to be well."

So it was that on the second Sunday in December 1659, in that remote and desolate corner of England, Richenda sat in silence in the great hall at Swarthmoor in the company of her mother and her stepfather and Margaret Fell and five of her seven daughters and her menservants and her maidservants—and waited upon the Lord.

It was a forlorn hope. She did not really think that she deserved to be graced. And yet, as the slow minutes passed and the silence grew, a joy beyond all imagining came to her. For a single ecstatic moment—between one pulse beat and the next— her world was shot with light. It was the briefest glimpse of a revelation. But it was enough.

When the three of them returned to their inn room that

night she knelt before her mother and her stepfather—as had been her custom in times past—and asked them both to forgive her for her churlishness during their journey north. But her stepfather raised her quickly to her feet.

"Richenda," he said gently, "you must never kneel to us again—nor to any man or woman—for we are all equal in God's eyes."

"Even parents and children?" she asked in wonder.

"Yes, even parents and children," he replied gravely. "Besides, my dear, it is *we* that should ask *your* forgiveness. We had not asked God's will concerning the marriage that we had planned for you."

Richenda turned to her mother. Was her silence one of consent?

Her mother nodded and smiled.

"It is true, Richenda, what your father has said," she answered.

"We will stay here a few weeks longer to learn more of the Friends," Mr. Bemmerton continued. "And then we shall return home to Benfield and await God's will concerning you."

7
❖ Richard Seeks His Fortune

RICHENDA and the Bemmertons returned to Benfield
on the very night that Richard threw the ox's liver into Obadiah's face. Thomas rode over to visit them two days later and,
on reaching home, sat down that same evening and wrote excitedly to Richard to tell him the glad tidings. Richenda was home
again, he wrote. And, best of all, she was unmarried. The wedding plans had come to naught. But the Bemmertons were not
cast down. They rejoiced. Something wonderful had happened
to them all in the North—which he could not explain. But why
did not Richard ride over from Oxford and hear their news for
himself? They longed to tell him. And he, Thomas, longed to
talk with him again. It was months since they had seen each
other. He wanted to hear about the university.

Thomas's letter had to wait for the carrier. And when it at
last reached Oxford, Richard had already left. He was ten
miles out on the road to London, his lute strapped across his
back—and his heart in his boots.

The farther he got from the accursed city of spires, the more
heinous his behavior at the university appeared to him. It was
like a bad dream. Yet it was worse than a bad dream, for he
was awake now; and he knew that it was a fact that he had be-

94

haved as badly as he had in the nightmare. He knew that his mother and his stepfather had indeed sent him those terrible letters. And that, in horror—longing to be rid of them—he had torn them into shreds and thrown them over Magdalen Bridge into the River Cherwell.

In the distance he could now see the blue line of the Chiltern Hills; and the nearer he came to them, the more insistently did memories of his boyhood at Benfield come pressing into his mind. Richenda's face—and Thomas's, too—no longer glimmered vaguely at him, as if through water; they were distinct and still. He could catch the tone of their voices and recall the way they smiled. What had bewitched him at Oxford? How could he have ever allowed so much to come between them?

In the evening, when he was well up among the hills and surrounded by the gaunt winter trees, he came to the drovers' track that led to Benfield and stood staring up it in utter misery.

Why, oh why had her parents taken Richenda away—just when he needed her so much?

Sick at heart, too ashamed of himself to go on to Maplehampden and find Thomas, he walked on through High Wickham and spent one of the few pennies he had left on a halfpenny loaf and the use of the ostler's straw for his bed at "The Three Pigeons" in Great Haddingfield.

Now the night he lay at Great Haddingfield happened to be a Saturday night, and since it was an offense for a man to be caught travelling on the roads on a Sunday—and he had got himself into such trouble with the world of late—he thought it wiser that he should spend the whole of the Sabbath in that ill-omened place.

In the morning, having been pitchforked out of the straw by the ostler, he took himself to church and sat there on a bench against the wall, his thoughts chattering as miserably as his teeth—for it was bitterly cold. What was going to happen to him, he wondered, if Dr. Boteler refused to come to his rescue and give him employment? Could he turn soldier? Or sailor? No master would take him as an apprentice, for he had no parent to recommend him or to pay the fee for his indenture. And he had not a single skill that he could think of, by which he was able to earn his bread.

What a fool he had been!

Now it so chanced that the minister at Great Haddingfield at that time was a kindly, good man who spoke of God's love and forgiveness. His text, Richard remembered for long afterwards, was taken from Luke 15, verse 20: *But when he was yet a great way off, his father saw him, and had compassion.* And the plight of the unhappy prodigal son, upon which the minister dwelled, being so like his own, he took comfort, thinking to himself that his own father—whose death he was said to have mocked—would surely not let himself be outrun by that father in the Scriptures. Surely he had forgiven him already.

At the sermon's end he was giving thanks for this and promising his father never again to offend him by his bad behavior, when a wild-eyed, long-haired fellow whom he had noticed before, sitting at the end of his bench, suddenly leaped to his feet and began haranguing the entire congregation.

"Poor foolish souls," he shouted. "Why seek you forgiveness in a steeplehouse built of stones and lime? Why seek you forgiveness in the emptiness of others' prayers and through a man no nearer God than yourselves?"

Richard was astonished at the man's outburst and even more astonished at the congregation's response. The people of Haddingfield, having received much comfort from the good minister's words—as had Richard himself—turned in fury upon the rude fellow and began pulling him out of the door.

"Christ's church lives not in steeplehouses nor in the mouths of priests . . ." cried the fanatic as they beat him over the head with their Bibles.

"Leave him alone, good people, leave him alone," cried out the minister from the pulpit.

". . . but in the hearts of men," yelled the wild man as they bundled him out into the churchyard.

As Richard followed the enraged congregation out of the church, he heard a great splash and then voices raised in angry jeers.

"What is it? What are they doing?" he asked a tall plow-man who stood in his way.

"Ducking the Quaker in the horse pond for his pains," he laughed.

"He's a Quaker?"

"He's troubled us before," explained an old woman at his side.

"A most meddlesome fellow," snapped a little shopkeeper with a sharp nose.

"A blasphemer, too," thundered the ostler who had let Richard sleep in his loft for the night.

Richard had often heard of these Quakers at Oxford. They were poor, ignorant folk, said some, whom the Devil had tricked into hearing voices and seeing visions, so that the crazed souls thought themselves messengers from God. Others called them stubborn, stiff-necked upstarts. And yet others considered them a dangerous breed of fanatics bent upon the destruction of the state. Whatever their quality or purpose, it was certain, men said, that these Quakers came out of the North and that their leader was a great, uncouth fellow from Leicestershire who preached to all and sundry in a stout pair of leather breeches and a leather coat and called his followers "Friends" and "Children of Light." The young undergraduate from Wadham who had taught Richard Euclid had told him that two poor crazy women belonging to their sect had greatly embarrassed their fellow Friends and caused grave offense to the citizens at their first coming to Oxford in 1654 by walking naked through the streets, whereupon both town and gown had set upon them and beaten them unmercifully.

"Let me pass. Let me pass," Richard begged as he pushed his way through the knot of churchgoers gathered in the porch.

He was all eagerness to run down to the pond to take his first look at one of so mad and mischievous a persuasion.

The young men of the parish were crowded round the pond, hurling clods of mud at the Quaker while he struggled in the water.

"Stop. Stop," cried the unhappy minister, running past Richard and grasping one of the young men by the shoulder. "You do not God's service in tormenting him so."

Richard could see now that the Quaker in the water was in a sorry state, for not only was he half drowned but he was also cut across one eye. His face was streaming with blood.

"Go home," cried the minister angrily to the young men. "Let the fellow pass on his way. It is not God's will that you should give him further hurt."

The young men slunk off unwillingly, and Richard was left alone beside the minister to watch the poor, mad creature stumble out of the pond and totter off to the far side of the nearby hedge.

"Leave him to himself," said the minister, turning sharply upon him. "And go your way, young man."

✳

Richard thought much about this first Quaker he had seen, as he trudged on towards London next day. He could not understand, he remembered long afterwards, how anyone should court being thrown into a pond for a mere whimsical notion that churches and ministers were not needful to religion. He was so hungry and cold and dispirited that he thought a man must be crazy indeed to raise such fury among his fellow men when all that anyone should ask of life was food and warmth and an honorable way to earn one's bread.

He was so empty in the belly by the time he turned from Cheapside into Wood Street that he would have turned Turk for a loaf of bread and a mouthful of the charred ox liver he had thrown in Obadiah's face.

As he stood before Dr. Boteler's house, he saw blobs of light swimming over the stout timbers of his door.

"So my young seeker-after-knowledge has turned brawler and malcontent!" exclaimed the doctor in anger.

Richard looked down at his feet. He could not bear to face his old friend's piercing eyes.

"You have been sent away from Oxford?"

He nodded again. He had told him how it was.

"Why, then, have you come to me?"

His blunt question was like a blow in the face. Richard felt stricken with shame that he must beg.

"Because . . . because . . ." he blurted out, "you said at Wittendon . . . in the smithy . . . that I should come to you if ever I wanted to study the natural sciences further."

"*You* want to study what *I* study?"

He nodded.

"Why?" the doctor whipped out.

"I thought . . . I thought . . . I thought, perhaps, I could be a physician, too."

"A physician!" Dr. Boteler thundered. "An unmannerly, foolish whelp like yourself?"

He told Richard roundly that to be a physician one needed self-discipline: a devotion to one's studies.

"Think you a physician throws offal in his teacher's face?"

Richard stared down wretchedly at his mud-caked shoes.

"Think you that a man of science runs after each new faction abroad in the land?"

His shoes, Richard saw, seemed a very long way off. He wondered how much longer he was going to be able to stand upright on his two legs if Dr. Boteler did not give him something to eat.

"Other men's politics," the old man continued, "and other men's religion are not the concern of the natural philosopher. A physician, such as myself, seeks only the truths of nature—and his patient's cure."

Richard must have stumbled or gone pale, for the doctor suddenly stopped his impassioned harangue and thrust his great nose close to his face.

"Go down to the kitchen," he barked. "Ask my folk to give you meat. While you are gone I will think what to do with you."

"How old are you?" he snapped, when Richard returned, heavy with food.

"Nearly sixteen, sir."

Dr. Boteler grunted in a manner that expressed his displeasure.

"A year too late to apprentice you off to an apothecary," he said sharply. "And you're spoiled—very likely—by the time you've wasted at Oxford."

Richard said that he hoped that this was not so.

The old man was sitting at his table, twitching abstractedly at the fur trimming of his long, old-fashioned coat, and scowling irresolutely at a whitened human skull that lay grinning at him from amongst his papers.

"Can you read Latin?" he shot out suddenly.

"If it's not too difficult."

He grunted again and began drumming his fingers on the table, clearly unable to make up his mind what to do. But then, to Richard's relief, he seemed to lose himself in thought, and, as he did so, his face relaxed and he began to look kinder. He glanced at him curiously.

"Do you still ask yourself questions, boy?" he inquired.

"About what I don't understand?" Richard asked, feeling happier now that Dr. Boteler was recalling their first meeting in the smithy. "Yes."

Richard nodded his head as he answered, and must—he supposed—have smiled.

"Why do you grin?" pounced the old man.

Emboldened by the good food inside him and by the doctor's changed mood, Richard forgot some of his fears.

"Because I do not understand you, sir. Nor why you keep a skull there on your table."

He did not like to add that he was also wondering what the man who had owned the skull must be thinking as he looked down from heaven and saw his head sitting among Dr. Boteler's papers.

The old man looked at him thoughtfully for a moment and then said gravely:

"I have always thought it good, Richard, for us men of science to be humbled by the remembrance of our latter end. It is healthful for us to remember that we, too, must die."

Then Dr. Boteler bade him sit on the window seat while he explained how things were with him just then. He was not a rich man, he said, for his practice of late years had fallen away sharply among families of fashion. He would not prescribe the popular remedies. He refused to prescribe millepede eggs for a case of anuria or to force live frogs down the throats of children to cure them of the thrush. He was a doctor, he said, not a magician. And, for this reason, he was too poor to offer Richard employment with a wage.

"I will, however, take you into my household," he said, "and begin to teach you what you ought to know. And you, in return, can help me in the writing up of my notes, in running to the apothecary, and in accompanying me on my visits to the sick and aged hereabouts in the city lanes."

Richard began to thank him joyfully, but the old man raised his hand.

"I shall be a hard taskmaster," he said sternly. "Make no mistake. I shall set you to your books early and late. And if after three months you do not make more progress than you would have done at Oxford had you been allowed to study for your degree in medicine, then I shall be as harsh as your step-father. I shall turn you out into the street. I will keep no idler under my roof. Do you understand?"

Richard looked into his sharp, bright eyes and nodded his head. He understood. And he was content.

Dr. Boteler was as stern with him as his word, for what with his learning his anatomy before breakfast, fetching drugs and studying in the *Pharmacopeia* all forenoon, dressing the doctor's patients' sores and visiting the sick and aged with him until supper, and writing to his dictation until far into the night —for Dr. Boteler was at that time composing his work on apoplexy—Richard had scarcely a moment to think of anything but the interest and terror of his new profession. Disease and death stalked them everywhere in that squalid city. And he was learning as swiftly as the raw soldier, new to battle, how sudden and implacable were their foes.

"We know so little, so little!" the doctor would mutter when hearing of a patient's death. "Our frail bodies are heirs to so many ills!"

Frail indeed!

The more Richard studied that strange bundle of bones, muscles, organs, arteries, and pipes which they called "a man," the more he wondered that any of them survived their birth. Life and good health seemed to him, in those first three months in Wood Street, the greatest and most miraculous of all human blessings.

He was lonely at times and often shot through with despair, for he was lost to Richenda forever, cut off from his friends, and still too unsure of himself after his great disgrace to feel hopeful about his future. Yet, in the thick of his day, he was not exactly unhappy. He was absorbed, rather, and stimulated by the new knowledge and the new thoughts crowding into his mind. And he was greatly excited by Dr. Boteler's original way of discovering new truths.

"Take nothing for granted, Richard," he said. "Observe

things for yourself. Weigh and measure every new phenomenon you meet. Then draw it. Write notes on it. That is the way to learn."

He said that he was sometimes glad that Richard had not studied medicine at the university, for then he might have had his mind cluttered with Aristotle and Galen.

"They were our fathers in medicine," he explained. "But we have outgrown these parents. And it is no longer right that we should look at disease through their eyes. We must trust to the evidence of our own."

And so he would teach his pupil about agues and fevers and tumors and gangrenes not so much from textbooks as from the living bodies afflicted with these ills. Richard's studies were a grim change indeed from his late pursuits at Oxford; but he could understand what he was taught and the purpose for which he learned it. And in their unequal fight against death, fought out daily in the London alleys, his wits—which had lain idle so long—came back to him a little and he began plaguing the old man with the same questioning with which he had plagued Marty in his childhood and the master at Wittendon in his schooldays.

"Why does an unclean wound cause a fever?" he asked. "Why does a man shake and feel cold after he has broken his leg? What makes us sweat when we are frightened or weep tears when we are sad?"

Very often Dr. Boteler was impatient with him, saying: "I told you that yesterday," or "Work that out for yourself; you are not a fool," or, very occasionally, "That is a childish question; it is not worth an answer."

But sometimes he would stop himself in the very act of snubbing him, pause, consider a little, and then look up, his eyes as puzzled as his pupil's.

"Yes, why? *Why*, Richard? I do not know."

And he would sit a long time afterwards, lost in hard thought, twitching at the trimming to his coat.

"There is so much we do not know," he would sigh at last.

It was an extraordinary time!

In that May of 1660, King Charles II came back to claim his own. And the people in the streets about them in the city rejoiced as drunkenly as the undergraduates had rejoiced at Oxford. They set up maypoles in the highways; they danced and sang far into the night. They lit bonfires, set off rockets, and rang the church bells. It was good to be alive to see such joy. In the midst of it, Richard thought of his friends with an ache. He longed to be with them; to know if Richenda were happy in her marriage; and to hear what the Bemmertons and Thomas and his father thought of this dramatic reversal of their fortunes. Life was like a seesaw. The Puritan cause was down. The Royalist cause was up. Up. High in the air. Sir James Egerton would recover his estates; Maplehampden could have a new roof. Best of all, Thomas could go up to Oxford and become the great scholar that he was so fitted to be.

"Are you not glad for the times, sir?" he asked Dr. Boteler one night as they sat up on the roof, taking the fresh air before they went to bed.

Scores of bonfires were blazing in the streets below them.

"I am glad, Richard," the old man replied gravely, "if the king brings us peace and justice and prosperity."

"But he has promised us these," he said eagerly.

"Rulers often promise more than they can grant."

Richard remembered that his master's caution dashed his spirits.

"It is order that we need most," the old man continued. "And an end to persecution. This poor country has been torn by religious strife too long. Men should cease tormenting their own souls and persecuting others' and begin to feed the starving children in the streets instead."

"But, sir!" Richard exclaimed, remembering the arguments he had heard all his life—both in his own home and at Benfield. "Surely it is right that men should attend to their souls' health, seeing that this life on earth is only a preparation for the next?"

"Fiddlesticks!" snapped the doctor. "Live your life honestly, Richard. Love God and love your neighbor. And leave the rest to the Almighty!"

❀

At last, fifteen weeks after Richard's coming to Wood Street, a letter reached him from Thomas. Thomas had written another letter to him at Oxford six weeks after the first, fearing that this had miscarried. Upon receiving no answer from this second letter, either, he had written him a third, sending it to Guildford, where the Drews now lived. Richard's mother had opened it and—after some delay—had sent word to Mrs. Bemmerton that she and her husband had disowned her son for his blasphemy and ill conduct at the university, adding that she neither knew nor cared what had become of him since.

"We pray God that we have found you at last," Thomas wrote. "Richenda and I fear that you are in great trouble. Come to us, Richard. Please come. We are your friends. The Bemmertons urge you to come. They say that your old room at Benfield awaits you. We could all help you to bear the grief that has come to you."

He continued by telling Richard what he had told him in his earlier letters: that Richenda had returned from the North unwed—that the marriage treaty had come to naught. He concluded with these words:

"If you committed blasphemy at Oxford—as your mother says you did—and you are truly sorry for it, then pluck up courage. Every one of us here carries the remembrance of a sin that is heavy to bear. If you cannot immediately come to us, then please write to your friend—Thomas."

Thomas's letter burst like sunshine into the dark house in Wood Street. Richard held his breath for joy. Richenda was free! She was no man's wife! He read the letter over and over again, not believing at first that he had read Thomas's handwriting correctly. Yet here it was: "She is unwed," and again, "The treaty has come to naught." There was no mistaking the words. Richenda was free!

And then, with this joy safely tucked under his belt, he read the letter a fourth time—and suddenly yearned to be with Thomas again. Thomas still loved him. Thomas had banished his shame. Thomas—to his amazement—rose up in his mind as someone infinitely strong and tender and certain.

Then, he read it a fifth time, and found fresh reason for gladness. Richenda feared that he was in trouble. Richenda urged him to come to Benfield. He read into the letter what he most wanted to read.

He wrote back to Thomas in haste, explaining his situation and sending each one of his friends his love. He promised to come to them as soon as he could obtain the doctor's leave.

Meanwhile the children in the lanes off Wood Street were stricken with a fever which Richard had noted before. First one family was ill with it and then ten more, until in three weeks it was so common and widespread that it fell as indiscriminately as the morning dew. The children's eyes were rheumy and they were blotched on their bodies with tiny rose-red spots no bigger than a pinprick. Six of them died.

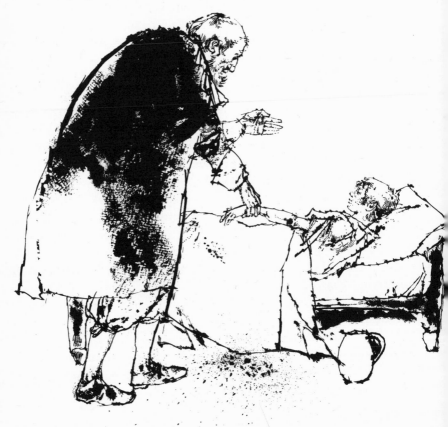

Dr. Boteler, when he came to them, took their pulses, looked into their mouths, and sometimes leaned down and put his ear to their chests. He bade Richard do the same. And, when he had looked carefully at some two score children afflicted with this fever, the doctor bade him describe their symptoms to him as carefully as he could.

"Well, sir," he replied, "the children start with a cold. And then their skins grow hot and their eyes become inflamed and sticky; and then they become blotched on the body with a red rash or measle—and this begins, oftentimes, behind their ears, which, sir, are often affected with pain."

His master nodded his head in approval.

"Go on," he said.

"Well, sir, most of them have a harsh, dry cough, and sometimes, when I listen, their chests make strange noises—as if they had consumption."

"Good. And their mouths?"

Here Richard looked puzzled.

"Well, sir, I think it is a chance that it is so . . . but . . . but I have noted . . ."

"Yes!"

"About the third day . . . the children have little white spots inside their cheeks. . . . But . . . these go away quite soon."

"Good. Good," he barked. "I see that you are learning to use your eyes."

That evening Dr. Boteler told Richard that he was going to examine him thoroughly on all that he had learned since he had come to him. The three months of probation were long over. It was now time to test whether his pupil was fitted to continue with his studies.

"But you have given me no time to look over my notes!" Richard exclaimed in alarm.

"No time!" he snapped. "What good is a physician whose knowledge stays all in his books? He must carry it here. *Here.*"

And he tapped his own forehead.

It was the most gruelling examination that Richard had ever endured, and made all the more alarming to him because so much was at stake. If he failed, he was out in the gutter. If he passed the doctor's test, Richenda was within his grasp; he had an honorable career before him.

What were the bones that made up the arm and the hand? the old man asked. And the foot? And the skull? And the rib case? Then he went on to muscles and arteries and veins. Then he took his pupil through the *Pharmacopeia* and asked him for what purpose he had asked Richard to gather foxglove and eyebright for him on the Chiltern commons, and for what conditions he would prescribe an infusion of sycamore leaves or the biting stonecrop. Then he inquired fiercely how he would treat a tertian fever. How gout? How a flux? Richard's head was in a whirl. The old man's study grew hot and close. Yet on he went. When should a doctor bleed his patient? he asked. When, on the other hand, should he give him nourishing diet and cordials? When purge him? When forbid him to drink? Richard stumbled in his answers. The white skull on the table grinned up at him, as if in evil jest.

Richard had no idea how he was faring, for Dr. Boteler only grunted at what he said—and sometimes scowled.

"And now tell me a physician's duty to those he serves," he rasped.

"Do you want me to recite the Hippocratic Oath?" Richard asked.

"What else?"

"I don't know it by heart."

"It's the matter I want. Not the words."

"A physician promises," he began hesitantly, "to . . . to adopt treatments which are only of benefit to his patient . . . and never . . . to . . . to give a harmful drug."

He came to a full stop, racking his brains.

"Oh . . . and he promises never to use a knife," he continued in a rush. "Not even on someone who has a stone. But . . . but to leave all surgery to . . . to the surgeons to perform."

Here Richard paused again.

"What else?"

"Well, sir, he . . . he promises not to gossip about his patients or their secrets."

"Nothing more?"

He was in a panic. He could remember no other clause in what he had learned.

"Does the young physician promise nothing else in the Hippocratic Oath?" thundered Dr. Boteler. "Has he no other duty to perform?"

Richard stared at him wretchedly. His mind was a perfect blank.

The old man got up from his chair, strode across towards him, and poked his long nose into his face.

"What, boy?" he asked fiercely. "Does the young student owe nothing to his teacher?"

Richard blushed with horror. What a fool he had been! He remembered now. It was the first clause of the oath. The very first! And the one that touched him most nearly.

"Yes, sir," he stammered. "He promises to revere his teacher . . . and . . . and to maintain him from want. He . . . he promises to look after him in his old age."

Dr. Boteler had turned from him in disgust and was standing with his back to him, his shoulders hunched.

He was undone! How could he have forgotten his gratitude —the gratitude of all students—to a good teacher?

The doctor would turn him back into the street. He was sure he would.

And then—unbelievably—he heard a low chuckle. The old man twitched himself round suddenly. And there he stood—his sharp eyes laughing at him in kindness and mirth.

"You'll do, Richard," he said. "I am satisfied. You have made a good beginning."

Richard stood staring at him, hardly believing what he had heard.

"You will . . . will keep me?" he stammered.

The doctor nodded his head. And then, since Richard still stood there—like a gawky boy—trying to recover from his success, the doctor addressed him sharply again.

"Don't stand there like a fool," he rasped. "The true man of science is surprised by nothing."

Then he added with a grin:

"Not even by his good fortune, Richard."

❀

Three nights later, as they sat on the roof, waiting for a cool breeze to blow up from the river—for it was early July by now, and the weather was very hot—the old man turned to him.

"You have worked well and done me service," he said. "And, since you have still much to learn and I want more of your help, I propose now to send you into the country for a space."

"Into the country?" exclaimed Richard, his heart beating with hope. "For what purpose?"

"A physician studies his student's health as well as his patient's," Dr. Boteler replied.

"But I am not ill."

"You are not bred to the close air and evil vapors of our capital," the old man replied. "You look pale."

Richard protested that he felt well and had no wish to leave him.

"Not even to journey into Oxfordshire?" the doctor asked slyly. "Come now, I can spare you for a little. The children's fever is past. Take my horse and ride down to your friends. And come again to me in the middle of the month."

Richard could not hold out against such joy. Indeed, he had no wish to, for the thought of coming again to Thomas and Richenda and to the Bemmertons filled him with a wild happiness.

"Thank you, sir," he exclaimed.

Next morning as he mounted the doctor's nag the old man stood close beside him in the street to bid him good-bye.

"And tell that girl at Benfield," he said quietly, "that she need no longer be ashamed of you."

8
✺ Benfield

H<small>E</small> rode that thirty miles through the summer countryside with the triumph of a king coming back into his own.
The young, pale harvest wheat was his, and the orchards green
with fruit, and the deep pastures and the trees and the distant
line of hills. England was his. He deserved her. What did it
matter that his mount was a sorry nag and that he had grievously outgrown his Oxford coat? He was happy. He was proud.
He had earned his self-respect. And he was going to his friends.

As he passed "The Three Pigeons" at Great Haddingfield,
he thought of his miserable night in the loft there nearly five
months ago. And when he looked across the village green at the
pond and the old church standing gray and stolid on its farther
side, he remembered the crazy Quaker he had seen dragged out
and ducked in the water.

"And so may all of that meddlesome breed be served," he
thought as he cantered on.

He and Dr. Boteler had seen much of the Quakers in the
city. Like many other members of the wilder sects in that extraordinary time, they ran through the streets prophesying
doom and destruction for the nation's sins. He and his master

thought they were poor, crazy, ignorant creatures for the most part—fitter for Bedlam than for liberty.

"They are spurred on by a dangerous pack of trouble-makers," the doctor said, "who seek to overthrow the State."

"How do you know, sir?" Richard had asked.

"Why, it is clear," he had barked. "They will not swear the Oath of Allegiance to the king. And they have a secret society with spies throughout the land."

The country had been vexed too long by damnable sectarians such as these, he declared. England needed stability, good government, and peace.

"And all true patriots," he concluded, "whether they fought for king or for Parliament in the late wars, should now support the new government and the restoration of law and order in our shattered realm. A pox on the Quakers is all I have to say!"

"A pox on all Quakers!" Richard shouted over the thudding of his poor nag's hoofs, as he left Great Haddingfield behind him and galloped joyfully along the lane to High Wickham.

Now Maplehampden lies three miles closer to London than does Benfield. And so, when he came to the first spur of the Chilterns early on that golden summer evening, he turned left through the beechwoods towards Hampden Hill, instead of carrying straight on towards Benfield and the Bemmertons.

"I will surprise Thomas," he thought. "I will tell him of my success. And we will ride on together to Richenda."

At each new evidence that he was approaching Maplehampden, he grew more and more excited. He was flushed with pleasure that he had passed the doctor's test, and he longed to share his happiness with the others. He longed to be again with the people he loved. Halfway down the steep lane to Maplehampden village he stopped at the gap in the trees to look down on Thomas's great house. There it was, far below him—looking just as he knew it would look—peaceful and beautiful among its green lawns beside the river. And there was the church, in which Sir James could now worship again as he wished, and the humps of the graves and the ancient, battered Egerton tombs. And the cottages and the ruined mill and the willows and the weir. It was all there. He heaved a sigh of relief. Below him, charted as in some old explorer's map, lay the country of his childhood—unchanged.

Yet, even in the moment of contentment, he knew that something was amiss. As he stared down at the dreaming house, he puzzled what it could be. Its trance was disturbing; it was almost deathlike. And then he realized what was wrong. There was no smoke coming out of its chimneys. The windows were shuttered. No spaniels lay stretched out in the sun in front of the hall door. Maplehampden was deserted.

He clattered down the lane, rode through the quiet hamlet, and tethered the doctor's horse to the post of the churchyard gate. There was a quick way over the wall at the back of the chancel. He had known it since he was a child. He leapt over the wall, ran across the lawn, and thundered on the iron knocker of the barred oak door, while all about him the shuttered windows of the great house stared down at him as sightlessly as the eye sockets of Dr. Boteler's skull. The sound of his knocking echoed far away through the empty rooms. He stood quite still, listening for the faintest sound of life from within: for the whimper of a chained dog or the mewing of a cat. But nothing came to him save the cawing of the rooks in the elms in the long avenue and the distant splashing of the weir.

And then, into the soft murmurs of the summer evening entered an age-old rustic crooning: "There, there, now. There, there," and the dull thud of a leathern bucket, and the sharp cackling of hens waiting to be fed.

Richard ran round to the poultry yard on the far side of the stables.

"Molly," he shouted to the old woman he found there. "Molly, what has happened? Where are Sir James and his son?"

Seeing him, her eyes lit up.

"Why, it's Master Richard!" she exclaimed, grinning toothlessly. "Master Richard, grown as tall as a tree."

And the old crone, thinking this a jest, started laughing and spluttering endlessly at her own wit.

Molly Rankin was as deaf as a post.

"Where's Sir James?" he bawled at her.

"Eh?" she asked, trying to guess his meaning by staring into his face. "Sir James?"

He nodded vigorously. The hens were all about their feet, clamoring for her to scatter the corn.

"Sir James's gone to Lunnon," she said in a loud, toneless voice. "Gone to the king's court. And 'is daughters 'long with 'im."

"And my friend Thomas?" he shouted. "He has gone with his father, too?"

She stared at him helplessly, moving her lips in answer to his own, but clearly defeated by her deafness, her age, and the angry pecking of hens.

"Master Thomas has not gone to London," came a quiet voice at his shoulder.

Richard turned. It was Molly Rankin's married daughter, Betsy Goode.

"Where is he, Mrs. Goode?" he asked. "I wish to see my friend."

She drew him away from her mother and the hoarse screeching of the poultry yard into the quietness of the empty stables.

"They left him here with the smallpox," she said.

"Smallpox!" he exclaimed. "Thomas has had smallpox?"

She nodded her head so grimly that Richard was suddenly gripped by the fear that Thomas was dead.

"He is not . . . not dead?" he blurted out.

Everything about Thomas that he loved rushed into his heart. Thomas could not—*must* not be dead!

The woman smiled faintly and shook her head.

"Master Thomas is not dead," she said.

"Then where is he?"

"With his friends," she replied dourly.

"At Benfield?"

She nodded.

He started to leave her, thinking to gallop straight off to the Bemmertons as quickly as he could; but he stopped, instead, and asked her:

"They left him? Sir James left his son while he was ill?"

Betsy Goode shrugged her shoulders.

"He wished to take his daughters to the king's court," she said shortly. "And there was me to bring Master Thomas his food and to change his clothes when the sweating took him."

Richard shuddered. He remembered his own illness as a child. And his mother's neglect.

"He was alone at Maplehampden?" he asked in horror, looking up at the blank windows of the great house.

Richard, at least, had had Marty.

"He had his friends," said the woman, pursing up her lips.

"They rode over from Benfield?"

"The young girl and her maid every day," answered Betsy Goode with a sneer which Richard neither liked nor understood. "The old people thrice a week."

There was no doubt of her angry contempt. It gleamed in her peasant eyes. How could anyone scorn such loving care? he wondered.

The woman suddenly turned on Richard a cold, distrustful stare.

"They're your friends, too," she said accusingly, remembering the past.

"Yes," he replied firmly. "They are my good friends. They have shown me much kindness."

"They have brought nothing but trouble to this house," she spat out.

"Trouble?" he exclaimed in astonishment. "What do you mean? What kind of trouble?"

"You'll find out soon enough if you're riding there," she said bitterly.

He rode along by the river towards Benfield with her words going round and round in his head. What could she mean? What had happened? As far as he could remember, Betsy Goode was not an evil or a jealous woman. So what had caused her anger and contempt? Was it just that she had mothered Thomas in his illness and had resented the coming of strangers? Could it be something as human and simple as that? But then why had she spoken of "trouble"? What "trouble" could Richenda and the good Bemmertons bring to anyone? All his life he had known them to bring only kindness and love. Was it, perhaps, just this? Had they protested against Sir James's bullying of Thomas and caused a breach between father and son? He turned this over and over in his mind. It seemed unlikely. Thomas was too patient and loyal to defy his father on his own account.

Then the obvious explanation of the servant's words burst upon him.

Thomas and Richenda had fallen in love!

Of course it was so!

And the Bemmertons, seeing their attachment—and themselves being fond of Thomas—had given their consent to the match. And why "the trouble"? Because that worldly old cavalier, Sir James, seeing how the king's return had mended the fortunes of the Royalists, had held out for a more illustrious bride for his heir. With Charles II on the throne, Maplehampden might aspire to the daugher of an earl for the mistress of the house. And Thomas—who would never have quarrelled with his father for himself—had done so for Richenda's sake. That was it!

Richard's heart ached. The whole bright evening seemed to darken in his mind. He realized now why no one had written to him from Benfield for the past three weeks.

As he cantered on towards his journey's end, not a breath of wind stirred in the valley. The quiet river and the empty marsh and the trees, heavy with their summer foliage, seemed to slip into a timeless dream. He remembered other summers and other rides: Richenda laughing; Richenda galloping fearlessly down the steep slopes of the hills; Richenda with her hair flying wild. It was all past and done with, now. It was all over—forever. Looking again to his left, he saw the gray willows leaning over the still river and the steady, glass-like reflection of their leaves on the surface of the water. Turning to his right, he gazed over the mown grass of the marsh grazing and up over the beech trees to the crest of Hampden Hill, where, long ago, they had seen the troopers out searching for the fugitive king. Everything about him was imprisoned in their childhood. In all the valley landscape, only he, Richard, was moving forward in the present; only he was in pain.

Then, as the river turned—and the track turned with it—he rounded the spur of the hills and saw them both, far ahead of him, riding together down the valley, as though they had set out from Benfield especially to meet him.

They were alone and they were happy. In the evening stillness he could hear Richenda's clear, bell-like laughter. The three of them were approaching one another quite fast. But Thomas and Richenda were busy in conversation, their eyes turned upon each other.

When would they look up and see who he was?

Richenda tossed the hair out of her eyes and looked straight ahead of her for a moment.

"Richard!" she shouted. "It's *Richard!* It's Richard!"

She spurred her horse and seemed to fly over the grass towards him.

"Richard!" shouted Thomas. "You have come at last!"

They sat on their horses panting, laughing, and looking at one another, while their mounts snorted and stamped, unsettled by their sudden gallop.

"You have been ill . . ." he began, turning to Thomas.

Thomas looked pale still, and thin; but his sickness was past. He looked composed.

"And you've grown as tall as a post," laughed Richenda, sizing Richard up.

"I am so glad you have come," said Thomas. "We were so anxious for you all those weeks that we had no news."

"And you can stay with us for months and months?" asked Richenda impetuously. "Do say that you can."

Richard explained briefly that Dr. Boteler had promised to train him as a physician and that he had to return to London in a fortnight's time. He made no mention of his recent success, for, somehow, it did not seem the moment to boast. He felt strangely disquieted still—despite their joy at his coming.

"We are so glad you have come," said Thomas again. "We feared that you might wish to stay away."

"Stay away?" he asked, feeling a growing hollowness inside. "But I told you that I would come. How could you think that I should wish to stay away from you all?"

A troubled silence fell between them.

"We are not the same, Richard," said Richenda at last, with a quiet seriousness he had never known in her before. "Not the same—as when you went away."

"How do you mean that you are not the same?" he asked foolishly, knowing all too well in what way they were different: they had fallen in love.

"We have become Friends, Richard," said Thomas with a taut smile.

Friends? So it was out. They were betrothed. His hopes were at an end.

"I am glad," he said firmly, trying to smile away his hurt. "I wish you both happiness with all my heart."

"Glad?" exclaimed Richenda, thunderstruck. "You wish us happiness? *You?*"

He was stung that she doubted his love for them both.

"But of course I am glad," he replied hotly. "When will you marry?"

"*Marry?*" exclaimed Thomas in astonishment. "We have not talked of marriage!"

"We are Friends, Richard. We have become *Friends*," repeated Richenda doggedly, her eyes bright with a desperate kind of courage.

Richard knew now what her words said; but he could not believe their meaning.

"Listen, Richard," said Thomas quietly. "Isaac and Susannah Bemmerton and Richenda and I—we have become Quakers."

Somewhere, high above them, a late lark sang in the primrose sky.

"We are not very brave Friends yet," Richenda was saying. "We could not give you our 'thee' and our 'thou,' Richard. We were afraid."

Her words came to him like the soft song of gnats.

They were Quakers! He could not bear it. He closed his eyes and felt sick.

In the darkness, he saw Richenda running naked down High Street at Oxford, like the poor, crazy girl six years ago. He saw her mocked and beaten and thrown in a ditch. He saw Thomas pulled out of a church and tossed into a pond. He saw his dear, good friends, the Bemmertons, running through the streets of London, prophesying death and damnation to the ungodly citizens of the new Gomorrah. He saw them buffeted by the jeering mob and pelted with the stinking refuse from the gutters.

"Why?" he cried. "Why have you done this thing?"

They spoke to him quietly of their convincement. Richenda and her parents had first met the Friends in the North, she said. They had seen the light. They had received God's message. They knew most certainly what it was that they must do in life. Thomas said that he had learned of God's will first through his friends. What they told him answered a problem with which he had wrestled for years. Then God, Himself, had spoken to him.

"But you are deluded," Richard said brokenly. "Your voices are leading you astray."

"No, Richard," said Richenda gravely. "We are not deluded. We have heard the truth."

He looked at them both quickly to catch the madness in their eyes. But now that their secret was out they looked singularly composed. They looked just like themselves. Like Richenda. Like Thomas. His friends.

And then he was suddenly gripped with anger.

"But Quakers are trouble-makers!" he burst out. "They are traitors to the king. They seek to overthrow the state. They . . ."

"No," interrupted Richenda passionately. "That is not true."

"We are a people who love peace," said Thomas.

Richard saw again the crowded, squalid streets of London; the disease, the poverty, and the violence of the great capital. He saw again the wild fanatics who ran, half-naked, through the city with lighted brands, their hair streaming wild and their eyes afire with madness. Then he returned to the three of them staring at one another in the fading light—distressed and angry in that quiet, green valley.

"You do not know what you have done!" he cried desperately. "You know nothing of this world."

"But, Richard," said Thomas with a gleam of amusement in his eyes, "it is not *this* world that we seek."

"It is in this world that you have to live," he replied bitterly. "And, in all ignorance, you have joined a stubborn, mischievous set of malcontents, bent only upon destruction of the realm."

"It is not true, Richard," shouted Richenda, her cheeks scarlet and her eyes blazing with rage. "Thou speakest false. Thou know'st not what thou say'st."

Thou! Thou! That little word startled them all.

Richard stared at her, horror gripping his heart.

Their world had cracked in two. A great gulf yawned between them.

"My son, my son," said Mr. Bemmerton gently. "We are a peaceable people. We come not with a sword."

"Then why, sir, does your sect disobey the law?"

Richard was filled with angry dismay that his old friends seemed so calm and stubborn in their foolish faith.

"Which law, Richard?" asked Mrs. Bemmerton mildly.

"The law of England," he replied. "All men know that Quakers refuse to swear the Oath of Allegiance to the king."

"Art thou angry, my son, because thou think'st us disloyal to the king—or because we will not swear?" asked the old man.

"Both," he replied bitterly.

"But thou art wrong. We are not disloyal. We will not *swear* our loyalty. That is all."

"Christ forbade us to swear," added Mrs. Bemmerton.

"Susannah is right," urged Thomas quietly. "It is in Matthew, chapter five, and again in James."

"*Swear not at all,*" quoted Richenda, "*neither by heaven . . . nor by the earth . . . neither by Jerusalem . . . nor by thy head.*"

"But Christ did not mean the Oath of Allegiance," Richard

persisted vehemently. "The oath is what all true subjects give their king."

"*Let your communication be, Yea, yea; Nay, nay,*" continued Richenda.

"And we give Charles our 'yea,' Richard," said Mrs. Bemmerton. "Indeed we do."

"The king is wise and good," said Mr. Bemmerton. "He has promised his subjects liberty of conscience."

"Yes," put in Richard quickly, "but Dr. Boteler says this freedom of worship is only for those who do not disturb the peace of the realm."

"But, Richard, we do not disturb the peace!" exclaimed Thomas.

"We live quietly at home," burst out Richenda indignantly.

"We are a peaceable people," Mr. Bemmerton repeated again.

Richard looked at the four of them—the dearest friends he had—torn between pity at their innocence and anger at their folly. How could he tell them that all men hated and despised the Quakers?

"Dost thou not believe us?" asked Mrs. Bemmerton, seeing his dismay.

How could he tell them that men spoke of the Quakers as blasphemers and atheists? That they feared them as enemies of the state? And that whenever Quakers met together in London there was tumult and affray?

"Richard," said Richenda sharply. "Answer my mother. Dost thou not believe what we have said?"

He was full of wretchedness. Everything about him in that much-loved parlor spoke to him of peace. The candlelight glimmered on the roses in the pewter mug, on Mr. Bemmerton's book press, on Richenda's hair. Thomas, sitting beside him, had stretched out his hand and grasped his knee—it was a thing he had often done when they had quarrelled or been at odds.

"I know . . . I know . . . you speak the truth . . . concerning yourselves," he said hesitantly. "But . . . but . . ."

"But what?" Richenda demanded.

Richard tried to explain that here at Benfield they were far from the world and did not know what men thought or did.

"Dr. Boteler—" he blurted out miserably "Dr. Boteler says the Quakers are a dangerous secret society—that they have spies throughout the land."

"Spies?" exclaimed Thomas.

"Dr. Boteler says that the government has intercepted their letters."

"Dr. Boteler. Dr. Boteler. Dr. Boteler," mocked Richenda cruelly. "Hast thou no mind of thine own, Richard, that thou canst only parrot thy master?"

Richard felt himself flush with anger.

"If I repeat what he says," he retorted in passion, "it is because he is right in his judgements. I trust him. He knows the world."

He and Richenda stared at each other almost in hate, while the gulf between them grew wider and wider.

In his anger, he turned upon Thomas.

"The Quakers are ignorant, stubborn bigots," he cried. "They spurn your Latin and Greek. They care nothing for your learning."

It was true. And, in shouting out the truth, he wanted to make Thomas as angry as he was. Thomas loved his scholarship. It was his pride. Richard wanted to make him lash out at him with his fists. He wanted to hurt him.

Instead, Thomas gave him a sudden smile—as though he had made a joke.

"But the Friends are right, Richard," he said. "Why should a man be a better Christian for knowing his Lily's Grammar?"

"Peter, the apostle, was no scholar," put in Richenda, scoring a point.

"Children, children," said Mrs. Bemmerton gravely, looking first at Richenda and then at Richard. "Let be. Sit in silence— till a better spirit comes to you."

They were not children.

Richard clasped his head in his hands. His whole life was going terribly wrong. He sat there in his darkness—in anguish —the smell of the roses coming to him from the pewter pot.

Richenda and Thomas were lost to him. He was in despair.

He left them early next morning, his love for them frozen inside him, so that he could not smile at Mrs. Bemmerton when she kissed his forehead nor thank the old man when he gave him God's blessing.

Richenda and Thomas rode with him to Maplehampden and they parted at the foot of Hampden Hill.

"Richard, Richard," pleaded Thomas, "do not go from us in hate."

But he turned away.

He did not look back at them as they stood by the forge, watching his ascent.

9
❀ The Gathering Storm

WHEN Richard and his horse had disappeared round
the last bend in the winding lane, Richenda burst into a storm
of tears.

"He hates us. Richard hates us," she sobbed.

She dropped her reins and covered her eyes with her hands
and wept.

"He is angry. He does not understand," said Thomas
wretchedly.

Richard's rejection of them was the worst grief that Richenda had had to bear since she had become a Friend, and the
pain of it had taken her by surprise. She could not believe that
such misery could come to her after so much joy. She felt as she
had always felt: that Richard was in some mysterious way a
part of her; that they were moved by the same forces; that
their hopes and passions—and even their follies—sprang from
the same source. And, now that he had gone from her in anger,
she felt that some precious, vital quality in her had been dis-
membered; that he had deliberately hacked away what it was
that bound them to each other; that he had disowned her, cast
her off.

Of all people in the world, she had most wanted Richard to

understand their new faith. And of all people in the world, Richard had failed them. He had turned from them in scorn.

Five months ago her convincement in the great hall at Swarthmoor had been as brilliant and startling as the flash of a kingfisher through a winter world. It had made her gasp. It had set the whole landscape throbbing. The wonder had held all through the long journey home. And—best of all—she had found it lying in wait for her at Benfield, seemingly even more radiant that it had appeared to her in the North. Every familiar muddy lane and sodden field and stark hedgerow was imbued with a new grace. She, herself, was different; she realized that. Ever since the moment of revelation her five senses had been strung to a new pitch. It was as though she had never seen things properly before, or heard them, or smelled and tasted and felt them aright. The fire in the parlor had glowed more warmly; the burning fir cones had smelled sweeter; at meal times, the bread and meat had had a new and delicious flavor. And at night as she lay in bed she had listened to the owls hooting joyfully in the woods and to the rain tapping gently on the window-pane, understanding for the first time that these—together with the multitudinous whisperings of the wind and the rubbing of tree branch against tree branch and the scuttling of mice in the wainscot—were the sounds of life. And that life was the most precious of gifts. With the slow unfolding of the spring, she had scarcely been able to contain herself. She had watched the beech twigs thickening into red bud and then bursting into the palest green leaf as though it were a miracle never observed before. And she had heard for the first time that the songs of thrushes and blackbirds were liquid and tumbling—like the mountain streams that she had met in the North. It was as though the whole world—and she, herself—had been born anew.

And now, Richard had cast them off! And she in her anger had answered him rudely—with all the old arrogance of former times.

"And I hate myself," she sobbed. "I hate to remember how angry I was with him."

"It is very hard to learn the patience of the Friends," replied Thomas sadly.

There was such unhappiness in his voice that Richenda looked at him quickly through her weeping, seeing four Thomases wavering and dissolving in front of her eyes. Then she dashed away her tears. Thomas was sitting on his horse, looking singularly solitary and frail, his face taut with grief. It was worse for him—far worse—she thought, suddenly overcome with the selfishness of her own distress. Thomas had not only lost Richard; he had also lost his own father—his whole family, in fact.

Richenda had been present at the terrible scene in the library at Maplehampden when Sir James had first learned that Thomas had joined the Bemmertons in becoming a Friend.

"A Quaker! You've turned a Quaker?" he had roared. "You whelp! You blackguard! You miserable, hypocritical rogue! I'll teach you to disgrace our name!"

And he had run out of the library, seized his riding whip, and, returning, had begun to belabor Thomas over the head and shoulders with the lash. Richenda had screamed and pulled at his coat-tails. Blood was streaming from Thomas's cheek. Then Thomas had quietly gripped his father's wrist, wrested the whip from his grasp, and had thrown the thing out of the window.

"Thou'lt not beat me out of my faith, father, so give over," he had said. "Thou tir'st thyself for naught."

"*Thou! Thou!*" Sir James had bellowed, beside himself with fury. "A pox on you, knave! You'll not 'thou' me in my own house! No, nor keep your hat upon your head before your father's face!"

And with a great lunge, he had knocked Thomas's hat off his head.

"Pick up your hat and take yourself to your room, sir," he had shouted. "I'll not endure a crazed, fanatic son in my sight —nor yet a traitor to my king!"

"I am no traitor to King Charles!" Thomas had expostulated.

THE GATHERING STORM · 127

THE GATHERING STORM · 127

THE GATHERING STORM · 127

"You're a traitor to your birth, sir. And to your country. Be gone. Out of my sight!"

And the enraged old cavalier had picked up a library chair to hurl at him.

Then he had turned savagely upon Richenda.

"Be off, baggage! It's your fault and your parents' that my son has taken leave of his senses!"

It had been a terrible time for Thomas—for them both. For Richenda had known that Thomas was confined to his room and denied his books. He was cut off from them all at Benfield and had to endure his persecution alone. She used to ride over to Maplehampden, and, being denied entry, would ride up the lane towards Hampden Hill and rein her horse in the gap in the hedge that overlooked the back of the great house. On the first morning she had waited for nearly an hour, hoping that Thomas would come to his attic window and see her there. At last he had come. He had opened the lattice and leaned over the sill and gazed and gazed at her, nearly a quarter of a mile away across the fields. He had not waved; but she had thought he had smiled. It had been enough. She had come the next morning and the next and next. They could not speak to each other; they could not even distinguish clearly the expression on each other's face. But the daily tryst had been a wordless pact between them; a comfort to both.

"But we must not despair," Thomas was saying. "No one ever told us that it was going to be easy being a Friend."

Easy indeed! Everywhere in nature Richenda saw the joyful assurance of their new-found faith; everywhere among men— save at home and with Thomas—she saw dissension and anger and unbelief.

For not only was there trouble at Maplehampden for Thomas but there was also trouble at Benfield for her parents. Two of their servants had hurriedly left their employment. And when her mother went her round of the cottages in the village she was met with frowning looks and the shutting of doors. It grieved her greatly, Richenda knew, for her mother was born to help others in the practical things of life, and it seemed as though her turning Quaker was now costing her this birthright.

"I think God will give us courage, Richenda," said Thomas with a sad, uncertain sort of smile. "I think that in time we shall learn to be brave."

"So your friends have turned Quaker, eh?" barked Dr. Boteler on the night of Richard's return to Wood Street.

They were sitting late in the doctor's study, his folk having gone to bed.

Richard nodded sullenly, disappointed that his old master had brought him no comfort in his grief. He had told him on his arrival why he had come back so soon, but, his servants being by, the old man had silenced him with a scowl and had turned away to his room. It had been a cheerless homecoming to him in his sadness. The doctor had wished to hear nothing of Benfield or of his journey—or even of his scrawny nag; and they had sat in silence throughout the evening meal, the old man scanning the proofs of his new book and Richard too dejected almost to eat.

"And that clever boy, too?" barked Dr. Boteler again.

Richard nodded, his resentment mounting.

"And the girl?"

"Yes," he snapped, bursting with irritation. "They are all turned Quaker. I told you so."

He could not bear that his master should probe his wound if he had nothing kind to say.

The old man eyed him keenly across the darkening room.

"Is it your vanity that is hurt, Richard?" he asked sharply, provoked by his pupil's rudeness.

His vanity?

"Is it that you are ashamed of your friends?"

"Yes," he blurted out angrily. "I am ashamed of them!"

He hated to think of Thomas joining himself with such low-bred fanatics as the Quakers and of Richenda shouting out her faith in the open streets—like any fish-girl crying fish. Their behavior disgraced *him*—their friend. He loathed their stupid *thee*'s and *thou*'s.

"It is the country that you should think of first," said Dr. Boteler severely.

"The country?"

The old man explained that though tens of thousands of Englishmen had thronged the capital to welcome King Charles back to his throne, there were tens of thousands of other Englishmen who had remained sullen and discontented in their own homes, fearful of the vengeance that the Royalists might now wreak on them and plotting—some of them—to overthrow the government before they, themselves, were destroyed.

"But the Quakers do not plot against the king," interrupted Richard hotly. "Mr. Bemmerton says his sect is loyal."

It was stifling in the room. It was stifling inside his own brain. He hated his friends for turning Quaker. And yet there was an unexpected twist in the strength of love that drove him fiercely to defend them.

"Pray God the government be so convinced!" exclaimed the doctor harshly. "But refusing the king his oath hardly convinces one of their love towards him."

"'Tis their conscience, not their love, forbids them swear."

"A pox on such whims!"

Richard hated Dr. Boteler that sultry night. He sat gazing through the dusk at his great beak of a nose, longing for a kind word or a whisper of hope that his friends might prove loyal. He was weary and sick at heart. He wanted comfort.

His master gave him nothing but a stone.

"The fools! The fools!" he exclaimed angrily. "To throw away their peace—the nation's peace—for a straw!"

Richard felt enraged and disgusted by the cynical old man.

"Suppose they be right?" he cried.

"How can they be right?" roared the doctor. "How can it be right to bring more trouble to this troubled land?"

"But they are *good* people," he shouted.

"The worse fools they," the doctor darted back.

A flash of lightning ripped the gloaming. The skull on the table caught its gleam. Then a thunderclap seemed to explode in the very room.

The noise battered the sense out of Richard's head.

"The worse fools they," Dr. Boteler rasped again, unmindful of the storm. "The worse fools they to bring the old chaos back again!"

Outside the window, the rain fell in sheets.

"The old chaos?"

"Richard, Richard," he cried impatiently. "For nearly twenty years we Englishmen have fought and persecuted one another in the name of religion. Is it not enough? *Enough?*"

"The Quakers do not persecute others. It is *we* who persecute *them.*"

"Yes," he snapped, "because in their stubborness they flout the one authority which can bring us civil peace—the king's government."

Richard felt hollow with despair.

"You mean they are a kind of traitor?"

"Yes. Of course they are."

Later that night, too wretched to sleep, Richard climbed out of the house—still heavy with the day's heat—and sat on the roof with his back to a chimney stack. He felt numb with grief and empty of thought. The storm had moved off, and over the hundreds of narrow gables and the city spires, the sky was clear; the roof-tops were gleaming in the starlight. In the night stillness, a faint wind fanned his cheek, bringing with it a hint of the distant sea. Looking down emptily at the great bend in the river, he saw the forest of masts and yard-arms of the ships at anchor—and thought of the bare beech trees on Hampden Hill in the winter.

He shivered. He felt the wetness of the tiles on his hands. He was cold.

One could go on living alone—to oneself—he thought dully, at last. There was fresh air and rain and the sea. One could live without friends. Without love.

And then, he gazed down on the squalid houses immediately below him and remembered the wretched creatures whom he and Dr. Boteler had tended in their sickness. He sighed. He still had his studies and his work. Richenda could not take these away.

In the coming year it proved even worse for the Quakers than Dr. Boteler had foretold. In October the Royalists sated their lust for revenge upon the Roundheads in the legal butchery of twelve of the regicides at Charing Cross. They were hanged, drawn, and quartered before a great crowd, and their blackening heads exhibited in public as a warning to the king's enemies. As much was to be expected—though it sickened Richard, used though he was to the dreadful consequences of human violence and disease.

"Man is the most disgusting of all the Creator's works!" exclaimed Dr. Boteler bitterly on the morning that the executioner cut Scot's and Scrope's entrails from their living bodies and held them up before their dying eyes.

Who now would dare to dispute the government's power to rule?

Yet, early in January 1661, Richard and the doctor were wakened one night by the furious sound of fighting in the streets. Some thirty-five fanatical sectarians who called themselves Fifth Monarchy Men had rushed out of their meeting-house in Coleman Street and had attacked the watch, crying, "King Jesus and their heads upon the gates." They were bent upon overthrowing the state and establishing Christ's kingdom upon earth by force of arms. For three days and nights London was in an uproar. And on the fourth, when the frantic uprising had been quelled and order restored again, the government issued a proclamation prohibiting all meetings of Anabaptists and Quakers and Fifth Monarchy Men and commanding the justices of the peace to tender the Oath of Allegiance to all persons brought before them for assembling at such meetings.

"It's all up with your Quaker friends, Richard," said Dr. Boteler grimly when he had read the proclamation. "If they refuse to swear that oath, they will find themselves in prison."

"Pray God, then, that they will not be so foolish as to attend a meeting!" exclaimed Richard.

It was a useless prayer. Richard realized how useless it was the moment that he had uttered it.

On that next Sunday—January 13, 1661—Richenda and Thomas and the Bemmertons and their three servants and Jacob and Prudence Newby, their neighbors from Hampden Ridge, sat in silence in the parlor at Benfield, waiting upon the Lord. Mr. Bemmerton had just spoken upon the subject of steadfastness. They must all have steadfastness, he had said. And the heart of steadfastness was a patient holding fast to that which was good: to their faith in God and to their loving-kindness toward all mankind.

"Let us pray for patience, dear friends. Patience that we may endure all things cheerfully and with courage."

Richenda knew that her stepfather was trying to prepare them for the persecution that lay ahead and was directing their thoughts to the plight of the London Friends who might, at this very moment, be being hauled out of their meetings and marched between guards to prison. She sat and thought of them with compassion, trying to imagine what *she* would do should rough soldiers break into the parlor here at Benfield and drag them from their chairs. Would she be able to contain herself with patience? she wondered. And—worse thought—would she be able to show the courage her stepfather had enjoined upon them? Would she not, rather, feel abjectly afraid? She hated violence; she had screamed and felt sick when Sir James had raised his whip to Thomas. And yet her own behavior in such circumstances was not at that moment an urgent fear to her. No one was going to test her valor on the instant. Benfield was far removed from London, and she and her parents lived so peaceably here—as did Thomas with the Newbys at Hampden Ridge —that she could not imagine that anyone would disturb them in their prayers that sunny, frost-bound morning.

She thought, instead, of the quality of "patience" and of how very unfitted she was in character to be a Friend. She was turbulent where she should be calm, and outspoken where she should keep her peace, and impulsive where she should be quietly resolved. But, worst of all, she had no patience. She wanted everything in a hurry; she wanted perfection to come in a moment; she wanted love and happiness here and now. She sighed. She looked across the room at Thomas, seated on one of the dining-room chairs, his arms folded across his chest, his head very slightly bowed in thought. She wanted to be married to him *now*. She had no gift for patience.

How easy it had been to tell Francis Norton that she did not love him and would never marry him! And how impossible it was to tell Thomas that she longed to be his wife! They were nearly seventeen. And she was sure that he loved her. What did it matter that he had no money save what he earned as Jacob Newby's amanuensis? What did it matter that Sir James was even now with the lawyers in London, trying to disinherit him? It was not wealth or even Maplehampden that they wanted. It was each other.

At that moment she caught a sound she had often heard before on winter mornings: the sharp ringing of a horse's hoofs upon the iron ground. It sent her mind darting back to the day long ago when she had listened to Sir James clattering through the village on his way to ask her stepfather to take Thomas as a pupil. She remembered that she had thought at first that the rider was a messenger bringing news of another war.

And then, her heart seemed suddenly to turn over in fear. It was not one rider! There were two, four, eight! A whole troop of horsemen was galloping up the avenue!

Thomas had lifted his head. His dark eyes were gazing straight into hers; they seemed to get brighter the longer he looked, till they appeared almost to blaze. He was talking to her across the silence with his eyes. What he was saying filled her with joy. He smiled. She smiled back at him. She was filled with a calm exaltation.

The soldiers reined in their horses before the house and noisily dismounted. They were swearing cheerfully at each other and making ribald jokes.

"Be steadfast," said her stepfather quietly, as the troopers burst through the front door and rushed shouting into the silent room.

10
❖ Thomas

SELDOM could the plighting of a troth between a man and a woman have been followed by so many months—so many years—of persecution, trial, and separation.

Thomas, and Isaac Bemmerton, and Jacob Newby were arrested by the troopers on that bitter January morning in 1661 and taken off to the Oxford jail. Susannah and Richenda and Prudence Newby stood at the front door and watched in silence as the sad cavalcade disappeared down the lime avenue. All three of them were valiantly trying to fight back their astonishment and grief.

"They are bearing witness to the Lord," said Prudence at last, with a catch in her voice.

"May the Lord go with them!" said Susannah firmly.

She was always at her finest in moments of stress.

Richenda felt the comfort of her mother's strength. But she could say nothing. Nothing at all. Her whole soul was in tumult. Thomas had stood up as the soldiers had burst into the parlor, walked across to her, and put his hands on her shoulders. Then, in front of them all and amid the shouting of the troopers and their overturning of the chairs, he had kissed her strongly on her forehead. Asking no one—not her mother; not

her stepfather—he had claimed her. He had kissed her not on the lips, like a lover, but on the forehead—like a husband. She was his. She could feel the imprint of his kiss even now; she could feel it glowing proudly there like a badge of honor.

And now, he was gone! Thomas was gone!

"What will they do to him, mother?" she burst out in despair.

Her mother turned and took her in her arms.

"Richenda, my dearest, we are all in the Lord's hands."

She stroked her hair gently over and over again as she had done when Richenda was a child.

"Do not fear for him," she murmured. "Thy Thomas is strong in his faith. He will not fail."

So her mother understood their love—and accepted it!

Richenda let out a long sigh that was half a sob.

Over four thousand Friends were torn from their homes in that bitter season and crowded into unlit, undrained, unheated prison cells, where their families were ordered to feed them. Though the Quakers were soon exonerated from all blame in the Fifth Monarchy Men's rising, many of them languished in prison until well on into the spring. Thomas and Isaac returned to Benfield from the Oxford jail in the middle of March, the old man shivering with ague and both of them looking physically worn out by the cold and filth of the prison. Yet their spirits were not only undimmed but seemed to glow brighter than ever before.

"We have met so many Friends," Thomas told Richenda excitedly. "So many good people who are strong in their faith!"

"There are more of us in the land—many more—than ever we knew," Isaac told his wife.

They described the meetings they had held, sitting in the snow on the balks of wood which were stored in the prison yard, and praised the goodness of the wives of the Oxford Friends in coming daily with bread and good cheer.

"My dears, we have been blessed in our afflictions beyond all measure," exclaimed the old man, his eyes glittering with fever and with the fervor of his joy. "In his goodness, God has shown us how many loving souls there be that travel with us."

Richenda and her mother had driven the coach over to Oxford in the early days of their imprisonment and brought sacks of flour and potatoes and two hams and the last of the stored apples to the wives of the Oxford Friends to help with the provisioning of the prisoners. But they had not stayed on in the city. There was work for them to do at Benfield.

"You must keep on with the meeting in the parlor," Isaac had urged them. "It is your duty, dear hearts. The light must never go out. Every first-day, you and Prudence and Hannah and Jane must wait upon the Lord."

All through the land, he had added, the wives and children of the Friends were keeping up the meetings. They must do likewise at Benfield.

And so neither of them had seen the terrible conditions in the prison in the third week of January, when more and more Friends had been thrown into the cramped dungeon, not for their supposed part in the late uprising—for which the Quakers had already been pronounced guiltless—but because of the cruel zeal of a local magistrate in tendering them the Oath of Allegiance. Since the Friends could not swear it, he committed them to the city jail. By the end of the month their dungeon had been an inch deep in water from the melting snow draining down into it from the yard above; and there were so many Friends crowded into this dismal hole that there was not room for them all to lie down at the same time. Only now, gazing into Thomas's and Isaac's pale and haggard faces, could the women glimpse the cruel privations that they had suffered.

"Isaac, my dear, my dear," Richenda's mother had wept, upon first seeing the frail old husband who had greeted her on his return.

"Thomas, thou art ill!" Richenda had exclaimed in grief, seeing the blue lines under his eyes and the skin stretched taut across his cheeks.

He was not ill, he had laughed. He was only very dirty, very tired, and in need of Susannah's wonderful meat pies. A night or two in a warm, dry bed would restore them both to health, he declared.

In Thomas's case, this proved true. The worst of his ill looks were washed away with the dirt. And in a clean set of clothes and with good food in his belly and fourteen hours of untroubled sleep behind him, he appeared not unlike the Thomas who had been arrested in the parlor nine weeks earlier.

Yet, in truth, there was a great difference. Richenda sensed it at once. The boy who had stepped across the parlor floor and had claimed her with such resolution was now a man. And his courage and strength had grown to man's estate. He was certain of his destiny. And he was certain of hers.

"Richenda, my dearest," he said tenderly. "We are betrothed

before God and before thy parents. And in time God will join us in holy marriage."

"In time?" she asked quickly. "Why not *now?*"

Yet she knew the answer even as she asked it. She felt sick with longing for him.

He explained that he had had much conversation with a hatter in prison at Oxford—a man who had travelled the country widely in the pursuit of his trade and who knew the temper of its people as well as he knew the quality of its hats. England was not ready for the message of the Friends, he said. It was too intolerant, too violent, and too much afraid. It was not just the government who were against them. Indeed, the king himself was not unsympathetic to their sect. The king wished all his subjects to enjoy the liberty of their consciences. It was Parliament and many of the common people who were their enemies. They longed for peace and for conformity, they feared religious strife, as well they might, seeing what terrible grief it had brought to England in their fathers' generation and remembering in panic the many hundreds of thousands of men, women, and children who had been slaughtered in Germany in the late religious wars.

"This hatter," he continued, "believes that many years of persecution lie ahead for the Friends."

"But, Thomas, he knows we come in peace!" she exclaimed in indignation. "We do not stop others worshipping God as they please. By our very faith, we could not start another religious war!"

"Why, yes, this hatter is one of us, Richenda. He knows what thou say'st," he replied gravely. "It is rather that our beliefs are so new to mankind that no one understands them. And what men do not understand they fear."

"And what is this to *us?*" cried Richenda, seeing clearly how it would be, yet clutching rebelliously at her own happiness.

"The Friends need us," he replied simply. "They need *me.*"

"Why thee?"

"Because I am not yet eighteen. I am too young to be tendered the Oath of Allegiance. The magistrates cannot imprison me upon the charge of not swearing."

He went on quickly to explain that the Friends' letters were being intercepted in the mail and that in the storm of persecution that was about to break over their heads there was a real danger that one little group of Friends might be cut off from the rest.

"John Freeman and Thomas Honor and Henry Smee at Oxford wish that I ride from one distant meeting to the next throughout these neighboring counties, carrying with me the tidings and the goodwill of them all. So will we face our testing, not alone and unknown, but with the help of one another's prayers."

"Thou must leave Benfield?" she asked, fighting back her angry tears.

He nodded his head.

Life was too cruel! Thomas had claimed her and had then been snatched away. And now, after those nine dreadful weeks of lonely longing for him, he was leaving her almost immediately. She felt bitterly disappointed with God that He should have ordained them such a parting.

"And Isaac?" she asked, clutching at a straw. "Does Isaac think that thou shouldst do what the Oxford Friends ask?"

He nodded again and smiled. Then he took her in his arms and kissed her.

"It is only a little while," he said almost gaily. "And we have so many, many years ahead of us to live to ourselves, Richenda."

She was ashamed of her terrible need for him. She could not bear that he should go. And she tore herself out of his arms and turned away so that he should not see how it was with her.

"Richenda, dearest, surely we can give ourselves to the Friends for a month?" he asked gently. "It is not much that they ask of us. In truth, it is not."

But it was not a month; it was nearly three and a half years before Thomas was free to settle with them again at Benfield. The need of the Friends for an active and discreet messenger —immune from the danger of being tendered the Oath of Allegiance—to travel between them and to shepherd the many new converts into the nearest fold was so great that Thomas was not at liberty to return to Richenda until late in September. And then, hardly had he been with her a day, when the Friends from Peter's Langland in Buckinghamshire sent for him to carry a long letter to Margaret Fell at Swarthmoor Hall asking her advice in a matter of conscience that had come between them at their meeting.

"Let me ride with thee," Richenda pleaded eagerly. "I would love to talk with Sarah again—and to see those lovely silver sands once more. Oh, Thomas, let us ride north together!"

Her mother would not hear of it.

"Not until thou art wed, Richenda, canst thou travel so!" she exclaimed, shocked that her daughter was so unworldly that she did not know such a journey to be improper.

"Then why can we not be wed?" she asked them all.

"Patience, my child. Patience," counselled Isaac Bemmerton, smiling gently. "Thou hast his love. Thou art sure of that. Canst thou not wait a little space to be joined with him in marriage?"

"I will come to thee again as quickly as I can," Thomas told her. "Indeed I will."

He kept his word. He returned to them late in October. But he came with a heavy heart, saddened that the Friends should demand so much of them both.

"Margaret Fell has asked that I go with the Friends into Holland," he said briefly.

"Into Holland?" exclaimed Richenda.

"But why thee, Thomas?" asked her mother. "Why must it be thee?"

"Because I can speak Latin," he replied.

"Latin! Surely the Dutch do not speak Latin?" asked the bewildered Richenda.

He explained that the Friends in England could not speak Dutch and that the Friends in Holland could not speak English, but that with his help and that of a Dutch scholar they could communicate with each other through Latin.

"I wonder what Richard would think of so strange a use for my learning," he said, smiling wistfully at the remembrance of his friend.

Then he sighed.

He would be gone most of the winter, he told Richenda dejectedly. They must try to be patient. They must try to remember that it was God's will that they were both doing.

"Is it not also God's will that we should marry?" she asked sharply. "Or is that a duty that must always come last?"

She was so disappointed and unhappy that she was cold with him at their parting. He had given his heart to the Friends, not to her, she told herself silently. There would always be journeys that he must go on. There would always be excuses. It was clear that he did not love her. She left him, booted and cloaked, standing in the hall, and went to her room. He could go his ways. He could go to Holland and talk Latin forever! He could ride away and never come back!

Then, hearing the groom bringing round his horse and the sound of his boots on the gravel and the faint jingle of the reins as he climbed into the saddle, she looked out of the window and straight into his white, disconsolate face. He looked shattered by grief. He looked suddenly small and young and without defense.

"Thomas!" she cried. "Thomas!"

She flew down the stairs and rushed into his downstretched arms.

"Oh, Thomas, please forgive me."

"Richenda, dear Richenda," he said, smiling uncertainly. "I love thee beyond everything in the world."

"I know thou dost," she smiled back at him through her tears. "And I love thee. I do, Thomas. I cannot live without thee."

He slipped down from his horse and took her firmly in his arms.

"When I return from Holland, I shall be eighteen. I shall be truly a man. We shall marry then, Richenda. I promise thee we shall."

She felt her heart overflowing with love for him. There was time enough, she thought. They were young.

"God speed thee," she cried gaily as he galloped away towards the village.

It was not in the power of either of them to keep that promise. The Friends were delayed in Holland until the end of April 1662. And by the time that Thomas set foot upon English soil again the terrible Quaker Act, passed by the House of Commons ten months earlier, had finally received the Royal assent. The moment that it became law Sir Richard Browne, the mayor-general of the city of London, at once ordered the arrest of all Friends attending meetings within the city bounds. Thomas, arriving among the London Friends on Saturday, May 4, attended a meeting with them at "The Bull and Mouth" the following day. The soldiers entered the quiet assembly with drawn swords in one hand and canes in the other. They dragged out the Friends, pulling the older men by their beards and kicking

the younger ones on the shins, beating all over their heads with their swords and canes. Then, with the coarsest of jests, they herded them through the streets and threw them into Newgate.

Richenda and her parents heard of Thomas's plight a week later, but they were given no time to come to his succor, for the very same day their own meeting at Benfield was raided and the three of them, together with Jacob and Prudence Newby and all their servants, were arrested and committed to prison.

It was a bitter, testing time.

Susannah and Richenda, for some reason that they did not understand, were imprisoned apart from the other women in a small chamber on the upper floor of a disused malting-house, the broken windows of which had been covered by sacking. It was a cold and gloomy place in which to be shut up and it smelled depressingly of damp and rusting iron from the flooded furnace house beneath them.

Richenda put her eye to a tear in the sacking and saw that the ground was only seven feet below.

"I could climb out of this prison, mother," she said, "as easily as I can climb out of the old mill loft at Maplehampden."

"Hush, child. Thou shalt do no such thing."

Susannah explained that they had been imprisoned by the law of the land. And since all Friends obeyed that law, they must stay where they were until the law released them.

They had a long wait. And in that time of waiting—deprived as they were of light, of warmth, of exercise, of bedding, books, flowers, and the thousand small duties of house and village, they came to know each other more freely and more closely than most mothers and daughters ever do. The barriers were gone; the generations no longer stood between them. Stripped of distractions and, in the gloaming, denied even clear sight of the other's face, they laid bare their souls in the long, dark nights, their voices rising and falling and keeping silence in a vast and empty world.

One night Richenda awoke, her shoulders aching from the hardness of the tiled floor, and turned over, seeking to find a more comfortable position.

"Richenda, art thou awake?" her mother asked softly.

"Yes, I am awake. How is it with thee?"

She hated to think of what her mother must be suffering in so cheerless a place.

"Shall I come to lie by thee and give thee my warmth?" she asked.

But her mother was not cold, she said. It was not her body that troubled her.

Richenda waited in silence.

"I am much troubled, Richenda," her mother began slowly. "Much troubled . . . in my soul."

The darkness seemed to press closer; it seemed to wall them in.

"Tell me," said Richenda softly. "Tell me . . . if thou think'st I can help."

After a long silence, her mother spoke again.

"It will grieve thee."

Richenda wanted to stretch out her hand in comfort to her mother, suffering alone on the other side of the darkness.

"It would grieve me . . . grieve me more," she said hesitantly, "if thou felt that I . . . I were not good enough to share thy grief."

After another silence, Susannah suddenly heaved her unspoken tragedy into her mouth.

"Richenda, I once killed a man."

Richenda could not believe that she had heard aright. The words made no sense.

"Thou hast killed a man?" she asked blankly.

How could her mother be saying such a thing? How was it possible that she could ever have killed anyone? Her mother? Her gentle mother?

"I shot him."

The three stark words exploded in the darkness.

"I shot him at Nettlesham. In the late war."

At Nettlesham!

Old Isaac's grief rushed back into Richenda's remembrance.

"At Nettlesham!" she exclaimed in surprise. "When I was a child!"

"Dost thou know of it already?" her mother asked in astonishment.

Richenda's mind was in a whirl. Her stepfather had left them alone—without protection. It had been a time of violence. Of sudden attack. He had left them alone—a mother and a child.

"No. I know nothing," she replied breathlessly. "Tell me, mother. Tell me what happened."

It seemed so quiet and safe at Nettlesham, Susannah explained. The house stood alone in its fields, which lay far from the roads, far from the tramp and toil of the war. Not a sound could they hear the livelong day save the lowing of cattle and the song of birds and the buzzing of bees. It was a haven of peace.

"And then, one night . . ."

Richenda could hear the shudder in her mother's voice.

"One night our herdsman came thundering up to our door. There were wild men in the valley, he said. They had set fire to the farm at Sutton le Field . . ."

In the darkness, Richenda listened aghast to her tale.

They had murdered the farmer and looted his goods. They had found his brandy and were now riding towards them, savagely drunk.

"Whatever didst thou do, mother?" she gasped.

"I unchained the door and pulled the herdsman in with us," she replied. "And he and I bolted the shutters and pulled the chairs and tables before the windows and doors. And then . . . and then . . ."

"And then . . . what?" she asked quickly.

"And then, Richenda, I looked at thee, lying in thy cradle. And as I looked and thou smiled, I heard the horsemen galloping up our lane . . ."

Brokenly, and in tears, she told the rest of the tale.

The drunken rabble had ridden round and round the shuttered house, firing off their pistols and swearing they would murder the people within.

"And I took Isaac's fowling-piece down from the wall, and fetched powder and shot, and went up to an upper room . . ."

She had stood at the window, she said, and watched the ruffians dismount and go to the barn and come again, carrying bales of straw, which they set against the door.

"Then one of them that had a torch came close to the bales . . . and . . . and . . ."

"Thou shot'st him," said Richenda.

"God forgive me," sighed Susannah in deepest wretchedness. "I shot him."

"What else couldst thou do?" Richenda asked starkly. "They would have killed thee and me and the herdsman hadst thou not done what thou dist."

"But, Richenda, I killed a man. I *killed* a man. I did not stop to persuade him from his sin. I killed him. I let him die in the midst of his wickedness."

In the silence that followed Richenda understood her mother's grief—and Isaac's also—to the very depth of her being.

No Friend took the life of another—even to save his own.

She felt through the darkness for her mother and came upon her tear-wet face.

"God will forgive thee, mother," she said brokenly. "I am sure He will. He knows that thou wast not then a Friend."

She tried to hide her own grief. She showed her mother nothing but tenderness and love in that long, unhappy night. But, deep down inside herself, Richenda was filled with consternation. The bright image of her quiet childhood was shattered into a thousand pieces. Everything had gone: her certainty in her mother; in her stepfather; in herself. They had lived in peace and grace with one another. And yet, behind them had lain this grievous thing—this killing of a man. They had all been living a kind of lie, she thought. When her mother slept at last, she sat propped up against the wall of the malting chamber and stared into the darkness, recalling one happy scene after another at Benfield in which her mother had shown her affection and given her the strength of her Christian example.

"And all the time," she thought, the tears rolling down her cheeks, "she was hiding this great hurt from me—and her soul's grief from my stepfather, too."

She realized suddenly that the guilt for the deed must have stood between her parents for years and years. Yet she, their daughter, had suspected nothing. Nothing at all. She had been blind and deaf and unfeeling to the true nature of things.

This childish incomprehension of hers caused her a more lasting distress than her mother's confession. It haunted her throughout the weary weeks of their confinement. Her mother had shot the man not to save her own life but to save her child's. It had been a desperate act of love: an involuntary, instinctive act, like a lioness defending her cub. But Richenda could find no such excuse for her own selfish obtuseness—her own unawareness of the true lives of people living so close to herself. She felt bitterly that she had in some way failed her mother.

In her remorse for her stupidity, she looked searchingly at her love for Thomas. Had she failed Thomas, too? Thomas was never long out of her thoughts at any time. But now that they were both shut up in prison—she in hers and he in his— and both enduring cold and hunger and darkness; and both, in a sense, alone—he seemed so close to her that she sometimes felt that she had only to turn her head to find him sitting beside her on the malt-house floor.

She had loved Thomas impetuously and selfishly. She had always put her need for him first. She had been self-indulgent in her passion. She saw that now. She had never clearly considered what it was that she could give him through her love, but only what he could give her.

"Thomas, I have been very childish towards thee," she would tell him silently. "Forgive me. I am older now."

At the end of August—perhaps appalled by the suffering of the Quakers or perhaps to celebrate the first coming of his queen to London—Charles II ordered the release of all Friends from imprisonment who were not ringleaders and who had not formally refused to swear the Oath of Allegiance in a court of law. Richenda and her parents, who had never appeared before a court, went back to Benfield. But Thomas, in London, was released one day and reimprisoned the next because he had earlier been tendered the oath and refused it.

The bitterness of persecution kept them apart for two anguished years more. It was a terrible time. No sooner had the king urged his government to be more tolerant towards the Quakers than some fresh Puritan plot against the throne was either revealed or suspected—and back went the Quakers to their prisons. The violence against them increased. Though they did not resist their arrest, the soldiers cudgelled them so brutally that one of them died. In prison itself they were treated more cruelly than condemned murderers and thieves; they were kept in waterlogged pits or caged up in narrow spaces carved out of the thick prison walls, or else—more commonly—they were so tightly packed into the common jails that, shut up at night, they nearly died of suffocation.

Hearing of the suffering of the London Friends in quiet Benfield, Richenda lived in an agony of fear for Thomas. She wrote to him almost daily and he wrote back, sending her letters which were both calm and cheerful.

"I am turned tailor," he once wrote to her. "All of us here in Newgate are plying a trade, and, since I have none, Abel Wright is teaching me to hem the linings for his waistcoats for him. Between us, we keep ourselves in bread, though, to tell the truth, I think Abel earns a loaf where I but earn a crumb. Fear not for us, dearest Richenda. We are in great heart and receive much strength from our meetings here in prison."

He told her nothing of the dreaded jail fever or that four of their number had died from it within the last month.

Early in the spring of 1664, Sir James Egerton died as he had latterly lived—in a drunken brawl. Isaac Bemmerton had been mistaken in thinking that the restoration of the king would mend his wits. It had done nothing of the kind. Sir James had sold what lands he could by law at Maplehampden, married his two daughters off to advantage, and then settled down noisily in London to a life of gaming, lechery, and drunkenness on the outer fringe of the court.

Thomas wrote to Isaac to tell him of his father's death and to ask him for his help in settling his affairs.

"Dear Friend," he wrote. "It grieves me to acquaint thee of my father's death. John Pierce brought me news of it two nights since, and this day my father's lawyer has been to me here in Newgate. The courts, he said, did not permit the disinheriting of an only son and I am, therefore, to inherit my father's Oxfordshire estates—and all his debts. Since I fear these be many and that he has not paid the servants at Maplehampden their wages for many months, I pray thee for God's love to ride thither quickly and relieve their distress. The lawyer says I have nearly a hundred pounds in ready cash, which he will remit to thee as soon as he can."

It was not Isaac who rode down the valley to settle Sir James's affairs, for he was crippled with rheumatism after his last imprisonment. It was Susannah and Richenda who paid his debts.

It was strange being at Maplehampden again—and on such an errand. The shuttered house seemed to stand before them in angry defiance, bearing the signs of its neglect as proudly as a spendthrift flaunts his rags. A chimney had been blown down; some of the roof tiles were slipping; and the grass had grown two feet high in the cracks between the terrace paving stones.

"We've had no call to keep the place clean—seeing no one came," said Betsy Goode sulkily as she handed Susannah the key.

They left the woman at her cottage, walked over the broken terrace, unlocked the front door, and entered the great hall. Here, they both stood speechless with awe. They had forgotten the portraits. They had forgotten that Thomas's ancestors would be waiting for them here in this shadowy, long-deserted house, staring down at them questioningly with their proud, dark Egerton eyes. There they were—six generations of them —from sharp-nosed, bony-headed old Sir Crispin in his close-fitting fifteenth-century cap and Sir Orlando and Sir Vivian with their pointed beards and ruffs, down to Sir James himself, painted as a young man in breastplate and helmet, girt to fight for his king.

"We ought never to have come," whispered Susannah.

They felt guilty—like people caught trespassing.

"It's Thomas's house, too," Richenda whispered back.

They crept past the portraits and up the creaking oak stairs, smelling the strange, sweet stuffiness of long-imprisoned air. As they wandered from room to room, a thousand memories stirred in their minds as they saw again the familiar chairs and tables and cabinets of glassware and stared at the gods and goddesses in the tapestries hanging on the walls.

"It is Mary's house, too," Susannah told herself, as they stood in the entrance of Thomas's mother's room. "I was beside her—holding her hand—at the moment when she died in that bed."

They climbed up to the long gallery. And here it was Richenda's turn to feel the terrible tug of the past. A shuttlecock was lying crushed and forgotten in the middle of the long, dusty floor. She stooped and picked it up and tried to straighten its feathers.

The three of us used to play battledore up here when it was wet, she thought sadly.

It was all over. It would never come back. Thomas was in prison. Richard was—God knew where. And only herself was left, standing here alone, and grieving for how it used to be.

Her mother walked over to one of the windows and unlatched it. The cold spring air flooded into the gallery.

"Richenda," she said robustly, in her old efficient way, "when thou be married to Thomas and hast this house for thine own, thou must be careful of the moths in the tapestries. And thou must see that the stairs be waxed. I noticed that the wood of the treads be cracking for want of its proper care."

Richenda smiled. Her mother was herself again.

But then, having smiled, she turned away, suddenly sick at heart.

How long would men continue to persecute the Friends? When would Thomas be freed from Newgate? When would they ever become husband and wife?

11
�֎ A Time of Joy

YET their long wait was nearing its end.

In July, Thomas was released from prison, gaunt and worn
by his long confinement, but wonderfully joyful in his inner self.
He felt so heavy and numb in his limbs that he could scarcely
hold his seat in the saddle, so he came to them at Benfield sitting in the bottom of Jacob Newby's cart, which was returning
from London after delivering vegetables and fruit and hams
for the imprisoned Friends.

"Thomas! Thomas!" cried Richenda, running out to meet
him.

He stood before her, dazed from his long jolting and smiling
all over his face.

"Richenda, I have come," he said foolishly. "I have come—
at last."

She held him tight in her arms as though terrified that someone would snatch him away again.

"Thou art home again," she gulped, between joy and tears.

And then, as she felt the thinness and the sharpness of his
bones, she quickly pressed down his head upon her shoulder so
that he could not see how stricken she was by his terrible ema-

ciation. He had stood there waiting for her in the forecourt looking like a ghost—a scarecrow.

"Thou art home," she sobbed. "Thou must never leave me again."

Never. He must stay with her for always.

He straightened himself up and gazed deeply into her eyes, his smile growing broader and broader.

"When shall we marry, Richenda?" he asked eagerly. "In a month? In a week? In a day? Let it not be long, dearest. We have lost so many years."

"Not in a day or a week," said Susannah gently, who was suddenly standing there by their side. "Thou must grow strong again, Thomas, before thou canst wed."

It was just as she said.

In that first fortnight back at Benfield, Thomas was so exhausted that he could scarcely stir from the house. The sun would heal him—surely the sun would heal him, thought Richenda, as she gazed, panic-stricken, at his weakness. She took him out into the garden and watched him smiling at the sky and the trees and the distant hills. He said nothing at first; he seemed content to sit in silence beside her, letting the sun beat down on his face, taking great breathfuls of the sweet summer air into his lungs, and just gazing lazily about him at the bees in the flowers and the birds flashing over the garden plots.

"Oh, Richenda," he sighed happily at last. "It is so good to be alive! So good to be with thee again—here in the country! In this beautiful world of living things! I think I have never felt God's goodness so keenly as I feel it now."

He would tell her nothing of the horrors of Newgate; of the stench and the filth and the terrible nights, lying cramped in his hammock, the other prisoners' hammocks swinging so close above and below and on either side that he could not turn over to ease an aching back. And the heat! And the lack of air! Men stifled to death in those sweltering summer nights. He told her nothing of this. She heard of it only afterwards from others. He spoke, instead, of the steadfastness of the Friends in Newgate and of the joy of their meetings when they sat together in the prison yard or on the dirty straw of the commoners' side.

"And, Richenda, it is very strange," he said slowly. "Our companions in misery in that doleful place—the thieves and the pickpockets and the murderers who are condemned to death— they no longer mock us as they used to. They do not disturb us at our prayers, as the soldiers do in the outside world."

Richenda sat beside him on the garden seat, smelling the heady scent of the newly trimmed box hedges and feeling Thomas's exquisite nearness and thinking about the criminals showing the Friends their respect, all at the same moment.

"Perhaps it is the nearness of their death," she said thoughtfully. "Perhaps men are kinder when they know they are about to die."

It was a golden time. Looking back, years later in her life, on the quiet, sunny days of Thomas's getting-well, Richenda could not recall a single word or deed—or even thought—with which she could reproach herself. She saw that her love for him matured and ripened with the slow beauty of natural things. As she watched the tautness going out of his face and his body clothe itself again in its youthful health, her happiness seemed to well up and overflow like a mountain brook.

"Thomas!" she exclaimed one morning, running to him eagerly in the garden. "Jacob Newby is bringing over the timber for the meeting house roof next first-day. Father has told me just now."

"And so?" he asked, looking up from his *Aeneid* and smiling at her excitement.

They had talked often of the new meeting house being built behind the barn at Benfield, rejoicing that in spite of all the persecution there were so many new Friends living in the hills and in the valley farms that Isaac's parlor could no longer contain them all. Lately they had walked daily through the farmyard and climbed over the stile to inspect the foundations being laid by Isaac's two menservants, Seth and Dick, and by such other neighboring Friends as could spare an hour's work in the evenings.

"Let us be wed the day that they raise the roof-tree!" she burst out.

She could see it all clearly in her mind's eye: the sun-swept hill; the flash of the distant river; the Friends standing in silence on the grass; her mother; her stepfather; Jacob Newby; Prudence; Seth and Dick; and a score of them more. And Thomas and herself standing together in the half-built meeting house under the roof-tree open to the sky, making their vows before God in their hearts.

She looked down at Thomas, expecting to find him as excited as herself.

Instead, he looked pinched with disappointment.

"But, Richenda," he said despairingly, "the roof-tree has to wait for the walls! They are barely two feet high!"

She slumped down beside him on the seat, suddenly as dispirited as he. At the rate that they were going, Seth and Dick and the Friends would take months and months to build them up to the height of the eaves. The vision of their wedding had come to her so goldenly—and now it was fading out of her mind like a dream. She had lost the radiance of it already.

"Richenda," Thomas exclaimed suddenly, throwing aside his book and jumping to his feet, "we'll build the walls ourselves!"

He held out his hands to her, laughing. She had seen earlier that they were much calloused by his imprisonment and strangely pricked about the thumbs.

"If I could turn tailor," he shouted joyfully, "I can turn bricklayer, too!"

He pulled her up almost roughly and hurried her out of the garden.

"Thou'lt see. Thou'lt see," he gabbled breathlessly as they ran through the farmyard. "We'll be married . . . before harvest home. We'll ride . . . to Maplehampden . . . as man and wife . . . before . . . before ever Dick has thatched Isaac's stacks."

He worked feverishly at first, mixing the lime and sand and water together and carrying the mortar to the wall and slapping it on, but he tired so quickly that Richenda took over the heavy stirring and lifting and left him to lay the bricks. It was a strange courtship, this moiling and toiling at the wall, yet right and fitting, too, for they were building a memorial to their love. They sweated and ached and laughed and grew tired together, their apprentice work made much sport of and so often set right by Seth and Dick that they might have despaired had they been in a less joyful scramble to get married. Yet the bricks were laid; the walls rose to the windows—to the top of the door. By the end of August they had reached the eaves.

On the next first-day—September 4, 1664—the Friends living in the Chiltern Hills about Benfield raised the roof-tree of their meeting house, and Thomas and Richenda became husband and wife before God and men. Isaac lent them the old coach and his two horses so that they could drive in state to Maplehampden.

They drove beside the River Thames over the open fields, the horses' hoofs kicking up the harvest dust and the wheels snapping the brittle stubble as they flew along. They were both so happy that they jolted and swayed together in the musty coach at first in raptured silence. Their whole lives—past, present, future—seemed suddenly caught up and suspended in that familiar, joyful journey to their home. They were husband and wife at last! Richenda knew that everything in her past life had been lived in order to fulfil this moment, and that—somehow —the people who had loved her: her mother and stepfather and the gathered Friends whom they had just left behind, were not *really* left behind, but were journeying with them, too. Every person and every event in her life bestowed a blessing on their marriage. She saw that even the bitterness of the long persecution had brought its gift, for she understood now most deeply the steadfastness of her husband's courage. She felt honored and humbled and overjoyed that such a man should love her. That they had snatched their happiness together out of a dangerous and cruel time lent a terrible beauty to the hour. The life ahead of them at Maplehampden might be short, might be anguished. They might both be arrested and imprisoned in a day, or a week, or a month. The future drove her back to the present. This drive along the valley was their own; no one could take it away from them. She looked to her right at the sunlight glinting on the river, and up on her left at the wooded hills; she smelled the dry sharpness of the dusty harvest field.

And the present took her back to the past.

"Thomas," she said quietly. "It was on just such a day that we once drove to Maplehampden when I was a child . . ."

She suddenly ached with sadness at the memory which the smell of the dust had stirred. Thomas looked at her, smiling gently, waiting for her to go on.

"The soldiers were out on the hills looking for the king."

"I remember!" he exclaimed, his face lighting up. "It was the first time I met Richard! I remember it quite clearly!"

"I was so anxious . . ." she continued hesitantly. "So anxious as we drove along."

"Anxious? Why wast thou anxious?

"I was afraid that Richard would not like thee—and that thou wouldst not like him."

Thomas laughed happily.

"Thou hadst no need to be anxious. We loved each other from the first."

The coach rounded the spur of Hampden Hill and they could see the chimneys of Maplehampden House over the tops of the sallows in the low grove.

"Dost thou think he will ever forgive us?" she asked sadly.

"For being man and wife?"

She shook her head.

"No. For being Friends."

Thomas did not answer straight away.

"Yes, Richenda," he said at last, "I think Richard will forgive us—in the years to come."

There was so much to be done at Maplehampden—and they had so little time! On the estate, as well as the season's plowing, thatching, and making safe against the coming winter, there were ditches to be dug to drain the sodden fields, fences to mend, stables, barns, and poultry yards to restock, coverts to thin, orchards to prune, and a new well to be sunk—all the small, necessary tasks which had been wilfully neglected in Sir James's latter years. In the house, Richenda found even worse evidence of decay. The roof was leaking over the top attics; the top of the great hall chimney had collapsed within its stack; and rats had gnawed a hole through the larder door. Yet by far the worst heartbreak that they had to bear was neither on the farms nor in the house, but in their servants' lost affection. Sir James had forfeited their respect by his wildness, and their duty by his long neglecting to repair their cottages and to pay them their wages. They scowled mistrustfully at Sir James's Quaker son and his Quaker bride. It was days before they nodded them both a good morning, weeks before they did their bidding without grudge, and a whole two months before they began to smile and hope that better days were come.

Richenda had brought to their marriage the income from her once-despised estate in Hampshire, and with this they began to repair the worst ravages of Sir James's spendthrift reign. The village street that November was littered with bright bundles of long-straw, as the thatchers set to work on the cottage roofs. One could stand by the bridge across the weir and listen to the threshers thumping their flails on the threshing floors and to the sound of axe and saw in the tangled woods among the hills. Wood smoke curled, fragrant and blue, into the autumn air. Thomas and Richenda, riding home in the cold dusks, would rein in their horses and stand listening to the new life stirring everywhere about them and smile at each other, at once proud and astonished that in spite of their inexperience thay had not failed Maplehampden and their folk.

Richenda was, in fact, perfectly amazed by herself. She spent cold, dank hours in the garden planting an herb plot, and riding over to Benfield for slips and cuttings and roots; she learned which were the best raspberry canes and plum trees to plant, and how to make poultices and salves and balms. She even began visiting the cottages—and found herself enjoying the visits.

"Goodness!" she thought one day. "I must be more like my mother than I knew!"

Yet, looking back on that winter many years later, it was not herself and her new duties that she remembered so vividly; it was Thomas. She saw him riding beside her round his estate and then reining in suddenly to watch a hedger busy with his hook and stick, his hands encased in thick leather gloves and his bush cutter on the grass behind him. Thomas asked the old man why he split the sapling ash and hawthorn as he did and how long it took to learn to lay a hedge as skilfully as he was doing; and the old hedger, delighted that his new master should take an interest in his craft, replied in a few grunting words, his face wrinkling into a strangely warm and unaccustomed smile. It was the same in the village street. The two of them stopped to watch the saddler and the wheelwright and the blacksmith at their work, and Thomas asked question after question, his dark, clever Egerton eyes darting here and there, noticing things that he had never even bothered to think about before. It was as though he had suddenly inherited a new kingdom—a country he had never visited before. They rode one sharp December day, she remembered, along the floor of the valley to the harvest field over which Isaac's clumsy coach had lumbered on their wedding day. A man was plowing it now. His horses strained at their collars as the plowshare cleaved the hard, resistant soil, their breath steaming up into the cold air. The dark lip of the turned soil, lengthening out behind the straining horses; the bright share; and the man guiding the plow, entranced them both. This was the austere, laborious beginning of the harvest year, the hard-fought, sweating battle between man and earth. They watched the plowman and his team drive almost to the water's edge and then wheel slowly round; the man scanned his furrow, spoke to the horses, and they were off once more, straining towards them, the dark ridge widening behind them.

"It's all in Virgil!" exclaimed Thomas, turning to her in his excitement. "It's all here—just as Virgil said! Here on my own estate! It has not changed at all!"

She smiled at him gently, marvelling that he had never watched a man plowing before.

"I think I have only lived in books up to now, Richenda," he answered with a laugh.

And in prison, she thought with compassion.

Her pride and joy in his awakening to his inheritance knew no bounds.

One day she told him so.

They had come in out of the winter dusk and were standing in the great hall. It was shadowy there, yet she was conscious —as she was always conscious—of the generations of Egertons looking down upon them through the fading light with their sharp, questioning eyes. She no longer felt like an intruder: she was there by right; their eyes said as much. And Thomas? Thomas was no mere appendage—like herself. He was their heir. Their glances were no longer quizzical; they were keen and amused and welcoming. Thomas had shown his love for Maplehampden and its hills and farms; he had shown his love toward their folk.

"Oh, Thomas," she cried, throwing her arms round him suddenly and then pulling him towards the pictures. "Look at all thy ancestors! They are smiling at thee! They are so pleased thou has come home."

Thomas stood under the portrait of old Sir Crispin and looked up thoughtfully into his crabbed, cunning, shut-in face. Then he shook his head.

"Not Sir Crispin, dearest. He does not smile. He could not have abided a Quaker for an heir."

Then they turned slowly to Sir Orlando and Sir Vivian, and Thomas shook his head again.

"They fought in Flanders for Queen Bess," he said. "Fine soldiers, both. Dost thou think they would relish a descendant who will not carry his sword?"

Then they stood sorrowfully and in silence beneath the portrait of the young Sir James. Here, the past was too close and too painful for them to speak of it.

"Richenda, dear heart," Thomas said at last, as he led her gently away, "we must comfort ourselves that we live for the future—not to please the past. We must thank my ancestors always for giving us so beautiful a heritage. And we must keep it so, not only for our children's sakes but for *theirs*. For the rest —we must forgive them their hate."

Looking back through the years, Richenda saw that it was Thomas's constant concern for the future—even his vision of it —that stayed most strongly in her mind. He seemed to regard Maplehampden and their two selves as mere instruments—unimportant in themselves unless they were used in the service of those who came after them.

"Dost thou not see," he asked eagerly one night after she had sorrowed at the cruelty of George Fox's long imprisonment in Lancaster Castle, wondering what good could ever come from such grief, "dost thou not see that we endure this bitter persecution not only for ourselves but for our children also— and our children's children?"

"What dost thou mean?" she asked.

"Why, that we suffer now that they may be free."

"In what way—free?"

"Free to worship God according to their conscience."

In his excitement, his words tumbled over each other. The Friends would triumph in the end, he said. They were bound to triumph. By their courage and their stubborn refusal to submit to tyranny, they would one day win freedom for all mankind to worship God in the way it pleased.

"*All* mankind!" she exclaimed, astonished. "Dost thou mean *everyone,* Thomas?"

He nodded and smiled, his face glowing with the vision of the future. Yes. He had meant everyone.

"But not Turks, Thomas. Thou dost not mean Turks!" she had said.

The Turks were even then sweeping far into Christian Europe.

"But of course I mean Turks, Richenda," he had answered her. "Why should not a good Turk or a good Chinamen or a good Red Indian worship God according to his conscience?"

This was such a new and startling idea to her that she had to take it away and think it over by herself.

"But dost thou not think it better to believe in Christ than in Mohammed?" she asked him next morning.

"Why, of course," he laughed.

Then were it not better to make a Turk become a Christian than to leave him in his error?"

"Not *make* him, Richenda," he replied earnestly. "Tell the Turk about Christ, tell him clearly, lovingly, and by example. But pray leave it to his conscience whether he follow Christ or no."

And then, early in January 1665, Richenda's cup of happiness was full. She was assured that she was pregnant.

"Dearest Richenda," said Thomas when she told him the news. And he saluted her with the same solemn kiss on her forehead that he had saluted her with when he claimed her at the meeting at Benfield long ago. "When will our child be born?"

"Early in September, mother says," she replied, smiling.

She smiled at herself as well as at Thomas, for she suddenly felt set apart from her former life, set apart, indeed, from all other women who had ever lived—as though bearing a child were a grace conferred upon herself alone. She felt at peace and fulfilled and infinitely thankful that God had made her as she was.

Thomas spoke of the child as of his golden future made flesh.

"He will live to see better days," he said, laughing. "He will reap where we have sown."

They told each other joyfully that the child's coming blessed their whole lives.

12
❀ London, 1665

FIVE months later, on a hot summer's day in the second week of June, Richard looked down aghast upon the first man he had ever seen to have the plague. Yes, it was the plague. He was sure of it. The glands in Mr. Fenton's groin had swollen to the size of an orange. He was in terrible pain. He was crying out in his agony. His pulse was low. He seemed to be dying.

"Lay back the covers upon him," he said quietly to the waiting woman.

Then he strode over to the casement, his mind in a turmoil, and stood staring down sightlessly at the familiar doors and shop-fronts of Wood Street. So the plague was *here,* he told himself in horror. Here, almost next door to them! It had leaped the city wall at last and had alighted in Wood Street. The plague was abroad in the very heart of the great metropolis.

Mr. Fenton groaned deeply. Then he cried out.

"It is the spotted fever, sir?" whispered the waiting woman, close at Richard's side. "Say it is the spotted fever?"

She looked at him piteously, her eyes deep as two wells.

"I think not," he whispered back, trying to empty his face of

his dread. "Try to comfort your master while I fetch Dr. Boteler. He will tell you for certain what ails Mr. Fenton."

He was about to leave the bedchamber and seek the stairs when he turned on the threshold and saw the woman standing there motionless in the middle of the floor, struck to stone by her terrible grief. He came back to her and took her hands in his own.

"Go to him," he whispered. "Let him see you sitting close beside him. It will give him strength."

It was all she could do, he told himself wretchedly as he stumbled, half blind with apprehension, down the dark stairs. It was all that anyone could do. There was no cure for the plague. No cure at all. No power on earth could stay it in its course.

The civil authorities had tried desperately to stop the infection spreading from Holland; they had quarantined ships and their cargoes and had looked askance at travellers from abroad. But the plague had slipped through their guard. It had appeared first in December in the parish of St. Giles-in-the-Fields, well to the west of the city and outside its walls; and by January it had spread slowly into the neighboring parishes of St. Andrew's and St. Bride's.

"And now it is *here*. Here in Wood Street!" muttered Richard over and over again—appalled—as he ran down the street towards his master's house.

Science had been no more successful than the civil authorities. It had been powerless in the face of the terrible scourge. The Royal College of Physicians had studied all means to stay the spread of the plague; it had published directions for cheap remedies for the poor. But all to no avail. The disease marched on.

"We know no cure," Dr. Boteler had shouted angrily at Richard one night. *"No* cure—and that's the end on't."

A wide farm cart coming up the narrow street, heavily laden with furniture, pressed him against a neighbor's door. An overhanging chest perched on top of the load brushed against the brickwork over the lintel, showering him with splinters of wood.

Everyone is fleeing, he thought, eyeing the passing treasures of someone's home. London is cursed. It is like Nineveh.

He hurried on, seeing again in his mind the dying man he had left behind and the ghastly tokens of the plague: the broken blood vessels round the edges of the swollen glands.

"We know no cure," Dr. Boteler had barked, "save what nature will work of herself."

"There are prayers and supplications," Richard had murmured.

The churches were everywhere crowded with people praying.

"Bah!" the doctor had roared in contempt. "What idiocy is it for us to live in filth—and then pray God to save us from our swinishness!"

"What do you mean?" he had asked, astonished.

"Why, Richard, if we really want to conquer the plague, we

must clean every filthy sewer in this filthy town, cart away the middens, sweep the gutters, kill every rat, every bed-bug, every flea . . ."

"But that's impossible!" Richard had gasped.

The doctor had shrugged his shoulders in a gesture of utter hopelessness.

"I know it is," he had snarled. "But 'twere better to try. 'Twere better to take out a spade and dig away a midden than to wear out the knees of one's breeches in useless prayer."

As they read the bills of mortality in the days that followed and watched the families thronging out of the stricken town, an anguished and irritable despair settled upon them both.

And now the plague had come to Wood Street!

Richard found Dr. Boteler in his study.

"Mr. Fenton has the plague, sir," he burst out. "I am sure he has the plague."

"*Our* Mr. Fenton?" exclaimed the doctor sharply. "Mr. Fenton of Wood Street?"

"Yes, sir."

"Quick, boy," he said, rising briskly to his feet. "The symptoms."

"Much pain, sir. And a great swelling in his groin."

"Tcht! From the beginning—as I have taught you."

"A giddiness, sir. His serving woman told me that he returned home on Thursday night staggering like a drunken man."

"And Mr. Fenton does not drink?"

Richard shook his head. The woman had told him how startled she had been to see her abstemious master so befuddled with wine.

"And then?" barked the doctor.

"He was ill all Friday with a fever. And today he was in so great a pain and so sweating and delirious in his illness that his woman sent for us."

"Very likely it be the plague," said the doctor somberly. "Poor devil! He was a good man. He deserved a better end."

"Will you please come, sir . . . and . . . and see for yourself?"

The doctor looked up sharply.

"Do you lack faith in your own judgement?" he asked.

"I . . . I have never seen the plague before."

His master gave him a sudden sad smile of understanding.

"Come, Richard," he said, putting his hand on his shoulder and gently propelling him towards the door. "We will go . . . go together . . . and look on the face of our enemy."

They walked down the narrow street looking—to any passer-by—like father and son. They had the same long nose, the same keen eyes, the same furrows graven deep down their cheeks. And, if nature's strange trick of repeating herself were not enough, Richard himself had added to the likeness, for, deeply devoted to his master, he had unconsciously adopted his gestures and mode of speech. He even tilted his head slightly backwards as he walked—as the doctor did—and surveyed the world sharply down the length of his nose. He presented a strange appearance for a young man of twenty-one, for his tall frame and sturdy build were at odds with the tautness of the muscles of his face. He had lost his former joy. The commonest expression in his eyes was a keen watchfulness; his full lips were set tight along the length of his wide mouth. He looked, somehow, like a gambler who had at one time staked all that he had, and lost, and who was now concentrating his whole being on another stake. He looked almost desperate to win.

"Does he cough much?" Dr. Boteler asked him concerning his patient.

"No."

"Are the swellings broken?"

"Not outwardly; but there is great inflammation and inward bleeding all about the groin."

The doctor grunted.

"Hot cloths and an opiate might relieve his pain," he said.

Richard nodded.

"So I had thought," he replied.

They came to Mr. Fenton's house and climbed the dark stairs, hearing above the faint groans of the dying man and the sobs of his woman. Then they entered, drew the servant gently aside, pulled back the bed-clothes, and stared down gravely at the vivid and unmistakable tokens of the plague. The patient's eyes were closed; he seemed scarcely conscious. Dr. Boteler felt his pulse and then sat down beside the bed and put his hand on his sweating brow.

"John," he said quietly, as one would wake a sleeping child. "John, it is I—Phineas, Phineas Boteler, come to see you."

Mr. Fenton's eyes fluttered open briefly and then closed again.

"I am dying, Phineas," he murmured. "Do you not think that I am dying?"

Richard looked keenly at his master, wondering how he would answer so difficult a question. Was it right for a physician to acquaint his patient of his coming end?

The old man did not hesitate—but he took his time. He held his hand still on Mr. Fenton's brow. Then he spoke calmly and with great compassion.

"I think, old friend," he said slowly, "that it is best that you should prepare for your death."

The dying man muttered something thickly, and the doctor, stooping to catch his drift, beckoned the woman to stand near.

"He wishes to leave you his linen and his draperies," he told her. "It is not in his will, he says. And take the twenty pounds that are in his cupboard."

Scarcely had he spoken when his patient's head suddenly rolled back, and Mr. Fenton stared sightlessly up at the embroidered tester of his bed.

"It is over," murmured the doctor, rising and closing the dead man's eyes.

As they were finishing their duty to the dead man, their duty to the living burst upon them. The woman shrieked, seeing her master dead, and buried her face in the curtains of his bed. Then she tore herself away and flung herself at Dr. Boteler's feet.

"Oh, sir, do not tell them," she cried, clinging to his long black gown. "Do not tell them that the master died of the plague."

Richard looked on, fearful of the doctor's cutting tongue.

But, instead of bursting out with cruel contempt, the doctor stooped and raised the weeping, frightened woman.

"You are Martha, are you not?" he asked quietly.

"Yes, sir," she sobbed. "I am Martha."

He put his hands on her shoulders.

"Look at me, Martha. Look at me hard."

The sobs came more brokenly and the woman stared hard at the doctor.

"Now look at my apprentice," he said, smiling gently. "Look at Richard."

The woman, in a kind of dream, turned and stared at Richard, too.

"We are your friends, Martha. Your good friends. We are your neighbors, too."

The woman looked from one to the other, dumb and confused, not really understanding what Dr. Boteler was trying to say.

"It is our duty as physicians, Martha, to tell the parish officers that Mr. Fenton is dead of the plague."

The woman looked as though she were about to shriek again, but the doctor held her shoulders tight.

"They will shut me up," she wailed in hopeless misery. "They will board up the door."

Dr. Boteler nodded, his eyes dark with compassion for her.

"They will board up the door," he agreed.

"And I shall be left alone," she cried. "Alone . . . alone in this great house."

Her voice rose to a shriek.

"I shall grow ill alone. I shall *die* alone!"

Dr. Boteler gave her a gentle shake.

"Have I not told you, Martha, we are your *friends*."

Her lips repeated his words soundlessly as though she were deaf; but she looked at him uncomprehendingly.

"My apprentice, here," he continued evenly, nodding towards Richard, "will come to your window twice a day and bring you food, and he will stay to ask for your health. You shall not lie ill alone. You shall not die alone."

The woman was whimpering now.

The doctor gave her another gentle shake.

"You shall not die at all," he boldly asserted. "Go now, Martha, and fetch another change of raiment. Take yourself to your kitchen, take off the clothes that you are wearing, wash yourself well, and dress yourself in the other clothes. My apprentice and I will burn what you are wearing in the yard, just as we shall burn the coverings and the hangings of your master's bed."

Martha listened to him spellbound, with her mouth half open —as though she were hearing the words of Merlin.

"Off with you now!"

That night, as he lay in bed, Richard heard the rattling of heavy wheels on the cobbles of Wood Street and saw the light from men's torches flashing fitfully across the ceiling of his room. It was the dead-cart come to take away John Fenton's corpse. Next morning, when he went to take Martha a loaf of bread and a can of milk, the parish carpenter was busy nailing up the lower windows. A watchman was already mounting guard at the door. He saw the woman standing pale and distraught at an upper casement. He waved at her, and she opened the lattice.

"Leave it on the sill of the parlor window, sir," she said dully. "I can reach it there."

He went away, sick at heart, thinking of the dreadful forty days before her—shut up alone in the house.

Three terrible months lay ahead of them.

In the same week that Mr. Fenton died in Wood Street another death from the plague was confirmed in Fenchurch Street and two more in Crooked Lane. The invisible enemy was indeed at work within the city walls. Yet matters were far worse in the parish of St. Giles, where over one hundred and fifty were dead of the plague in a week. The disease had crept along the foul ditches into Westminster, and the king, close by at Whitehall, decided to move to Hampton Court. Once the king had gone, no one stayed who could with a good conscience leave. Civil servants, lawyers, brokers, and merchants hurriedly packed up their travelling chests and went to their friends in the country. Eastwards in the city, Richard had to push his way on foot to his patients past traffic jams of coaches, carriages, carts, drays, and even barrows—for it was becoming difficult to hire a horse. And, glancing up one morning through the lattice of a patient's bedchamber on London Bridge, he saw that even the Thames was being used as a route for escape. The river was crowded with hoys, shallops, skiffs, wherries, and pleasure boats carrying people away from the stricken town.

Only the poor will be left, he thought swiftly. The poor and the sick and the dying—and such as attend upon them.

For, surely, the physicians and the clergy would not desert their charges.

Through that breathless July the sun rose hot and clear every dawn and beat down pitilessly out of a cloudless sky. Richard had never known such heat. Paint blistered; wood cracked; and the leading on men's roofs grew soft. The garbage thrown out into the gutters rotted and stank within the hour, and hundreds of thousands of small flies hovered and hummed over the middens and the open drains. Day after day the carpenters were out nailing up the stricken houses and painting scarlet crosses upon their doors; hour after hour the bells tolled in the city belfries. By the end of the month the pestilence was raging so fiercely in the neighborhood of Wood Street that Dr. Boteler and Richard could no longer spare the time to work together. Dr. Boteler took the early morning hours in his consulting room, tending the people who came to him with undressed sores, strange feelings of numbness, fluxes, headaches, and all the nervous afflictions caused by the terror of the times, while Richard went abroad to the households already known to be visited by the plague. The watchman, knowing his profession, unlocked the doors, and he passed within to the sweltering, eye-smarting fumes of saltpeter and vapor of vinegar and burning leather and rags—anything to smoke out the infection in the air—and climbed the dark stairs towards the screams of the delirious and the sobs of those watching helplessly at their sides.

"God help us. God help us, he said over and over again to himself as he dressed sores, incised swellings, and washed and fed and tried to comfort his patients.

When he came to think of it, this calling upon God was very strange. For Richard did not believe in God. Yet what else could he do? What else could he say? All about him men were fighting a ghastly and a losing battle against an enemy that they could neither see nor understand. And he, who had been trained to defeat just such an enemy, found himself useless and unarmed. His scalpel did not heal; his poultices did not cure; his drafts did not even deaden the terrible agony of the disease. Those few who survived their fearful ordeal did so, he thought, in spite of his skill.

"Drink up your sack, boy," barked Dr. Boteler when they sat

down to their midday meal. " 'Twill keep out the infection. Drink it up, I say."

Then forth they went again, Richard to give out anti-plague water to the crowd of wretches clamoring at the doctor's door, and the doctor himself, his gold-headed cane in his hand, to walk through the emptying streets to the parish pest-house to dress the sores of the inmates there.

On and on they worked, day after day, their fatigue sharpening their tongues, and men's anguish driving them nearly to despair.

"The vicar of St. Giles, Cripplegate, has quit his post," croaked Richard indignantly across the supper table one night. His voice was hoarse with tiredness.

"He's no worse than the heads of our own profession," the doctor snarled back.

The old man looked gaunt and overstrung from long watching at men's deaths.

"What new physician has left town now?" rasped Richard.

He felt brittle and tense. He had long felt forsaken—deserted by all that he had ever learned. One more betrayal and he would strike out in rage—or break down in tears.

"Is it not enough that the president of the College of Physicians has taken to his heels?" flared the doctor bitterly. "And two of the physicians and two of the surgeons at St. Bartholomew's Hospital?"

It was a sorry tale.

"And now it is Thomas Sydenham," said the old man brokenly. "Thomas Sydenham . . . in whom I had . . . so much trust."

It was a daunting hour. The deaths from the plague had risen to two thousand a week; and Richard and the old doctor had supped full of horrors in the pursuit of their profession. Yet the plague itself had come from God, or the Devil, or rats, or fleas, or from the air. It was not of man's making. But now, in this supreme moment of testing, man was everywhere revealing himself to them as a monster, a creature more cruel, dastardly, heartless, and base than either of them—cynics though they were—had ever dared to fear. Not only had parish priests

and doctors deserted their duty, but thousands of employers
had fled the city, leaving their servants behind them, penniless
and without lodging. Parish officers were driving men and
women, stumbling with the plague, out of their own parish into
the next to save themselves the expense of burying them. Friend
forsook friend in the street at the first sign of a faintness or a
shivering in the limbs. Every man lived for himself alone. Kindness and loyalty and trust lay gasping on a death-bed more terrible than that of the plague.

That night Dr. Boteler was called to a house close by, in
Cheapside.

"Do you go," said the old man to Richard. "I am over-
spent."

"But—but it is in Cheapside, sir," Richard replied hesitantly.
"It . . . it must be some rich merchant."

"So?"

Then the old man smiled wearily.

"Aye, there will be a good fee. You can keep it, boy. You de-
serve it."

It was not a rich merchant who was ill. It was his young wife,
left alone in the fine house with her old serving woman and a
boy of twelve, who had come for the physician and who now led
Richard down Wood Street and to his mistress's door. He
climbed the stairs behind the servant, hearing no groans from
above and no evidence of the sickness save the sweet smell of
wood smoke, which suddenly—achingly—took him back to the
parlor at Benfield on winter nights.

The old servant opened the bedroom door and, handing Richard the candle, pointed to the bed.

"My mistress lies sick of a fever, sir."

Not a sound came from the bed, but as he stooped by his patient the light fell on her face and she opened her eyes.

"Dr. Boteler?" murmured the girl, for she was scarcely as
old as himself. "I had . . . had thought thee . . . to be
older."

Her words came slowly as though it were difficult for her to
drag herself out of her silent anguish. Richard explained that
he was Dr. Boteler's apprentice and that he had come to exam-

ine her for her illness, at which the girl shrank from him, not in terror but in an excess of physical shame. She turned away her head, and he heard her sob.

Suddenly he understood.

"I am a physician, madam," he said gently, "before I am a man."

The girl's swelling was under her left arm. It was large and angry and about to burst.

"Fetch me hot water and many cloths," Richard said sharply to the servant. "Quick. Do not tarry a moment."

The girl rolled her head slowly from side to side and sighed —a valiant containment of the agony she was enduring.

"Your husband?" asked Richard quietly, after he had taken her pulse. "Does he know that you are ill?"

The girl continued to roll her head.

"He must not know," she whispered. "He must not know. Thou must not tell him."

"Why must your husband not know?" he asked angrily. "And where is he? Why is he not here by your side?"

"He is in Newgate," she whispered.

"In Newgate!"

His surprise had slipped into his voice.

"We are Friends," she murmured. "He is committed to prison for our faith."

The servant had returned with the cloths and the hot water.

So they are Quakers! They are Quakers! thought Richard as he prepared to lance the poisoned gland. They are at one with Thomas and Richenda! Memories of his two friends flooded into his mind. He saw them as he had left them—sad and yet loving, at the foot of Hampden Hill.

And then the courage of the sick girl beside him and the calm competence of the servant and the brave dignity of this stricken house stole into his heart. *This* was the way to meet the plague, he thought. Here was a family that did not disgrace mankind.

He lanced the swelling and gave the girl such ease from her torment that the tears rolled down her cheeks.

"I thank thee. I thank thee."

She shut her eyes to stop the tears, but they welled up under her lids and continued to roll down her face in a steady stream. "You will feel more comfortable now," he said, smiling.

But he told her also that she was still very ill, that her crisis was not over. He would watch with her through the night, he said, for he must dress her arm. And she must try to eat and to drink a little wine to fortify her strength. The servant went down to the kitchen to do his bidding in preparing food, and he stooped and wiped the sweat from the girl's brow and dried her tears with a dry cloth.

When he had finished she opened her great eyes and looked at him steadily.

"It is the plague that I have?" she asked.

Richard nodded his head.

"It is the plague," he replied.

She lay back quite calmly at first, accepting the confirmation of her fears. But, after a moment, she frowned and began to stir.

"Rachel!" she cried out in distress. "And Tobias! What will happen to them now?"

"Your servant and the boy?"

"Will they not catch my infection?"

She was in a fever of disquiet.

"You must be calm," he said firmly. "And you must lie still. Do not fret for your servants."

"But for me . . ." she began brokenly.

"They must take their chances," he said.

Everyone in London had to take their chances. Even Dr. Boteler and himself.

"We will not forsake either you or your servants," he continued. "One of us will come to you every day in your quarantine."

The servant returned with wine and broth and fed her mistress while Richard stood at the closed casement looking down upon Cheapside and watching the hateful procession of men bearing torches, heralding the arrival of the dead-cart. The dreadful cry, "Bring out your dead. Bring out your dead" came to him dully as though from a long way off through the thickness of the leaded panes. Looking back at the quiet scene at the bedside, caught in the circle of candlelight, in which the old servant was feeding her mistress, spoonful by spoonful, and crooning at each sip, he felt most deeply the contrast between what lay outside this house and what lay within. He knew that warm blood was coursing about his heart; the muscles in his face went slack; he felt almost dizzy with relief. For here—in this Quaker household—were love and duty and grace. Here was comfort. Here, in the abyss of his despair, he had found hope.

"I have a friend who is a Quaker," he suddenly blurted out. "Thomas Egerton of Maplehampden. Do you know him?"

The girl's eyes lit up.

"Thomas?" she said, smiling. "Why, he was with Rufus for many months in Newgate. We know Thomas well."

She murmured she was glad that he was safe in the country now and far from the plague—and blessed with the happiness of a wife.

"A wife!"

"Why, yes," she exclaimed in wonder. "Didst thou not know? He and his Richenda are wed at last."

So Thomas and Richenda had married after all!

"Last September, it was," put in Rachel unexpectedly. "For it was then that John Smee rode down into Oxfordshire for the raising of the roof-tree of the meeting house at Benfield."

Married! They were man and wife!

All night, Richard sat by his patient's bed, watching her doze and tending to her poisoned arm when she stirred, thinking endlessly of his two friends and pondering on what might have been. Yet he did not grieve. Their happiness and their safety were a comfort to him. Their love for each other was a haven, a sure anchorage, in this storm-tossed, howling night of the world.

"God bless them both," he said to himself—and then smiled. marvelling that the words came so naturally to his lips.

Thomas and Richenda had need of blessing, for that same night they stood facing each other in the parlor at Maplehampden, bitterly unhappy and torn by strife.

"Thomas, Thomas," Richenda cried in terrified fury. "Thou canst not go. Thou canst not!"

She was so shaken by passion, so full of dread, that she clutched at the table to save herself from falling.

"Thou *canst* not go!" she cried again.

Thomas stood white and drawn and so wretchedly unhappy that he could not look her in the face. He had turned away his head.

"It is the Lord's will," he repeated doggedly—despairingly —for he had already told her this a dozen times.

"How *can* it be the Lord's will? It is madness. It is the Devil, not God, that tells thee so."

This great horror had come to them first in a cloud no bigger than a man's hand. They had followed the news of the plague in the capital through the months of April and May and June with aching hearts and fervent prayers. They had sat in silence in the meeting house at Benfield offering their souls to God and beseeching Him to deliver the London Friends. And, after each first-day, Thomas had returned with her across the fields, his face looking whiter and more drawn with every passing week. And then, in July, with the deaths from the plague rising higher and higher and the plight of those left behind in the city growing daily more terrible, Thomas had taken to crying out in his sleep. On waking, he had clutched at her and flung his arms round her desperately—as though some enemy were trying to tear her away. And later, when she rose and went about her daily tasks, he had followed her, dumbly, foolishly, watching each slow movement with tortured eyes.

And now, at last, it was out!

"The Lord bids me go to London, Richenda," he had told her ten minutes ago. "He bids me bring comfort to the Friends in Newgate."

He had laid aside his book, looked at her long in silence as she hemmed the infant's gown, and then—gently and slowly— spoken the words that had murdered her joy.

"What good canst thou do?" she had cried fiercely, once she had grasped the full horror of what he had said. "They are in prison; thou art powerless to prevent their deaths."

"If it is God's will," he had replied humbly, "I might bring them hope."

Nothing would alter his terrible decision. Not her panic for him. Not her anger. Not even the pitiable nearness of their coming child.

"It is His will that I go, my dearest," was all that he would say. "It was His will that I should go three weeks ago."

He had denied God's call, he confessed sadly. For a whole twenty days he had turned his back upon what God had asked him to do. He had stopped up his ears. But now he must go.

Richenda clung wildly to the heavy oak table. Her whole world seemed drowning in grief before her eyes.

"Thou wilt catch the infection, Thomas," she cried out in anguish. "Thou wilt catch the plague."

She knew in her heart that he must go, that he must act upon his conscience, however terrible the task that it set him to perform—or else Thomas would no longer be himself. He would no longer be the man she loved. And yet, when she thought of him entering that city of dreadful night—when she thought of the ghastly nature of the illness to which he was exposing himself—she cried out again.

"What if it is the Devil that is tempting thee, Thomas?"

Her voice was shrill with fear.

He turned upon her sharply.

"Richenda, thou know'st it comes from God," he said with passionate intensity. "And thou know'st that what *thou* say'st comes not from God but from thy fear."

She bowed her head. She knew it, indeed. Her fear that he should catch the plague and die—be torn from her in the very flower of their love—engulfed her in a wave of despair.

"If thou diest," she gulped, "how can I live without thee?"

He took her quickly in his arms.

"I shall not die."

But she could not be comforted.

"If thou diest," she sobbed, "how can I endure the years till I can come to thee again?"

"Richenda, dear heart, I shall not die. We must trust to the Lord."

He told her, then, that while he had sat with her that night summoning up courage to tell her God's will, he had opened the

Bible to find words to give him strength and that the book had fallen open at the 91st Psalm.

Her sobs came brokenly as she listened to what he had to say.

"Come," he said gently, "Let me take thee to thy chair and I will read to thee what the Lord put it into my mind that I should see."

And Thomas read her these words:

Thou shalt not be afraid for the terror by night; nor for the arrow that flieth by day. Nor for the pestilence that walketh in darkness; nor for the destruction that wasteth at noonday.

"Go on," she whispered.
And he continued:

There shall no evil befall thee, neither shall any plague come nigh thy dwelling.

She dried her tears slowly and then sat in silence for a little, holding his hand.

"We will go to London together," she said quietly. "We will set out tomorrow morn."

"But, Richenda!" cried Thomas in horror. "Thou canst not! Thou art carrying the child!"

"I am not married to the child!" she flared. "I am married to thee!"

Her tears broke out afresh. They were man and wife, she cried. Where he went, she went. If he faced danger, then she should face it, too. And face it at his side. They were married. They were one flesh. Neither God nor man should keep them apart.

It was not so, he replied in anguish.

"Richenda, thou hast had no call from God. The Lord has not told thee that thou shouldst go to London."

It was true. And the truth tolled like a bell within her heart. She was torn with hopeless grief.

"Surely it is the Lord's will," he said tenderly, "that thou stay here and bear our child in safety at thy mother's home?"

"At Benfield?" she asked drearily—all passion spent.

He had written to Susannah, he said. He had asked her to fetch her to Benfield on the morrow.

Richenda clung to him, weeping, when they went to bed, overwhelmed by their cruel plight. She was too exhausted to hate the child stirring within her, who was separating her from Thomas—and too full of wretchedness to rail at God. She was adrift in a terrible sea, battered by mountainous waves.

And she clung to her husband as a drowning man clings to a drifting spar.

When she awoke, Thomas had gone.

13
❀ The Lord Have Mercy
upon Us

DURING the following week Richard snatched stray moments out of his nightmare days to think of Thomas and Richenda.

So they were married!

He saw them, in his mind's eye, walk up from the river hand in hand, cross the greensward, and enter the beautiful house. Now they were standing in the great hall under the eerie scrutiny of the portraits; and now they were in the library and Thomas was talking about his books. It pleased him, as he hurried through the desolate streets, to think of Thomas as master at last in his father's house—a credit to his forebears, albeit a Quaker. A rich man furnished with ability, living peaceably in his habitation. And then, suddenly—as so often happened in those terrible months of the plague—Richard was transported back to the green places of his childhood: to Benfield; to the beech-covered Chiltern Hills; to the banks of the Thames; to Maplehampden. And now, in brief reverie, he was chasing Richenda up the Maplehampden stairs with Thomas close behind him, while Sir James thundered at the three of them from below.

"I wonder if they still hid in the broom cupboard?" he asked himself foolishly as he dressed a patient's sore. "I wonder if they still play at shuttlecock and battledore in the long gallery when it rains?"

And then he sighed. The attic chamber was fetid and stifling. The streets were stifling. Overhead, the sun beat down out of a brazen sky. When, in this terrible summer, would it ever rain?

As he had promised, Richard continued to attend the young Quaker wife in her sickness and found that his visits brought him a rare comfort. For the girl was mending. With care, she should live. Her slow recovery was giving him back his faith in medicine, just as the patient dignity of the girl and her two servants was giving him back his faith in human nature.

One morning, as he was leaving this household and pondering upon the unhappy irony of his now respecting a sect which he had once so bitterly scorned, he looked down the length of deserted Cheapside and saw in the distance the figure of a young man approaching him from the direction of the poultry market. Something in the set of the head and the way the young man swung his arms made him pause a moment. Then he shrugged his shoulders, turned his back on this lone traveller in the dying city, and set off on his return to Wood Street. It was strange, he thought, how one's eyes deceived one: how they summoned up the likeness of the very person one was thinking about in the face of a mere stranger.

He was tired, he remembered. He had sat up until dawn with a dying child. He had not slept a whole night in his bed for the past three weeks; and he was walking back to Dr. Boteler's at a laggard's pace. Suddenly, into his drowsy thoughts of the patient he must visit next broke the sound of running feet. He turned. The young man was hurtling down Cheapside towards him.

"Richard!" gasped Thomas. "It is thee! I knew it was thee!"

Richard gaped at him, too tired and too astonished at first to trust his senses.

"Thomas!" he exclaimed, at last.

He stared at his friend. Thomas was a man. Not a boy. A lightly built, tight-strung, eager-faced *man*.

"Thomas, why are you here?" he barked sharply. He was suddenly panic-striken for this man. "Why are you not safe at Maplehampden?"

Thomas reached out both arms impulsively to embrace him. But Richard drew himself back quickly out of his reach.

"Don't!" he shouted fiercely. "Don't touch me, Thomas. My hands—my clothes! I have sat with the plague—all night—all day."

He read something of his own wolfish gauntness in Thomas's dark eyes.

"Thou hast been overtired," Thomas said gently.

But he kept his distance. And they stood there in Cheapside, staring at each other across ten feet of empty street, reading swiftly with their eyes the checkered histories of five long years.

"Thou need'st not fear," said Thomas, smiling his shy, uncertain smile. "I have come even now from the pest-house. If God has willed that I catch the plague, then I shall have caught it there, already."

"The pest-house!" Richard heard himself croak. "You have been to the pest-house?"

Thomas explained that several of the Friends had become infected and had been taken to the pest-house. There were still more of them, he said, who were sick of the plague in the prisons. He had come to London to bring them what comfort he could.

"But *you?*" Richard cried out. "Why *you?*"

The thought of Thomas and Richenda safe at Maplehampden had been his greatest solace in the last terrible few days. They had been his hope. His hope of a world beyond the plague.

"*No man is an Island, entire of itself,*" Thomas was murmuring shyly.

"And Richenda?" Richard found himself shouting in anger. "You have not brought her, too?"

He could not bear to think of Richenda abroad in this city of sudden death.

Thomas shook his head.

"She is safe at Benfield, awaiting the birth of our child."

Richard, in his tiredness and anxiety, felt himself trembling on the edge of tears. Richenda was pregnant! And Thomas had left her! Left her at such a time! And to come to such a place!

His anger with Thomas drove out his grief.

"You ought never to have come," he said harshly. "You ought never to have left her at such a time!"

Thomas looked suddenly as though he had been whipped across the face. He looked sick with pain. He turned away his head and stared at the gutter.

"And what good can you do here, now that you are come?" Richard continued cruelly. "You do not know how to nurse the sick."

Thomas looked up quickly.

"But that is why I have come to thee, Richard," he said earnestly. "That is why I have to come to Wood Street this morning."

"Why?"

"To ask thee and thy master to teach me what I should do."

Richard stared at him, watching his lips moving, not understanding at first what he was saying. Then, as the words broke through into his tired brain, he suddenly felt himself gripped with anguish. The whole image of Thomas stood before him— not just the strained, eager young man standing ten feet away in the street, but Thomas the smudge-eyed child so tautly afraid on the weir bridge, Thomas at school diving naked into the filthy pond, Thomas gabbling with delight over his Homer.

"You wish us to teach you how to nurse those stricken with the plague?" he heard himself ask.

Thomas nodded his head.

"Then, follow me," his voice said.

He was racked by his anguish. The true horror of the plague had touched him at last. Someone he loved had come within the city's bounds. Someone he loved—had always loved—was now in the Foul Fiend's clutch.

Thomas—voluntarily, heroically—was putting himself into the same mortal danger as Dr. Boteler and himself. He could not bear the waste.

✸

As Richard led Thomas up the stairs into Dr. Boteler's study, Richenda—twenty-five miles away at the foot of the Chiltern Hills—turned to the driver and bade him halt the cart.

"Thou must go no farther, Jacob," she said. "It is here thou must leave me."

She spoke the truth. Fifty yards ahead of them across the London road stretched a road-block guarded by soldiers. She knew—everyone knew—that the soldiers had orders to shoot all persons fleeing from the doomed city who tried to force their way through into the country. She and Jacob had come to the point of no return. Once past the road-block, there was no driving home to Maplehampden

Jacob looked at her in dumb distress.

"I . . . I . . . cannot leave you, mistress," he blurted out at last. "I cannot let you go alone."

Richenda turned to him, her eyes blazing.

"Thou canst!" she said forthrightly. "And thou shalt!"

She seized the reins out of his hands.

In the gray dawn, Richenda had ordered him imperiously to load up the cart with vegetables and flour and cheeses. She had bullied him, taunted him, battered him with words to drive her out of the valley and towards London. He did not understand such a woman. He was afraid of her.

"Go now," she said urgently. "Take thy way back through the fields. Thou wilt be home before milking."

She drove on past the road-block, her head held high, deaf to the protests of those who would dissuade her.

"Let go!" she flashed at a soldier who made a grab at her horse's head. She raised her whip to him. "Wilt thou keep a wife from her husband?" she cried fiercely.

She was alone now on the empty road to London—alone in a countryside burnt brown by the pitiless sun.

In her solitude, she found calm. She was at peace.

When her mother had come to her on the morning that Thomas had left, she had felt too frightened for Thomas and too forsaken by him to hide her grief. She had wept and wept in her mother's arms. But, after the weeping, the grayness of exhaustion had descended upon her, dulling her pain. They had walked together to the herb garden which she had planned and planted last winter and then wandered down by the river and along its bank to the dilapidated mill. Everything that she had seen that morning had spoken to her of Thomas.

"Mother," she had said, "I will stay here at Maplehampden a little longer. It is nearly a month to my time. I will stay here a little longer in our home."

And her mother, seeing her calmer and knowing what she had said to be true—and divining the comfort to be found in the surroundings which one loves—had replied:

"I shall send to thee daily, dear child. And thou shalt come to us when thou wilt."

There had been no deceit in Richenda that morning. She had spoken as she had felt. Yet, as the days passed and the remorselessness of their fate was borne in upon her, her longing for Thomas had grown to an intensity that she could no longer endure. What is life without him? she had thought, panicked. It is death. Not life.

Heavy with child, she had wandered on foot through the August heat and dust round the Maplehampden fields. She had stopped at the hedge where they had spoken to the hedger nine months before; she had stared at the dry wheat heads growing where they had watched the plow. "Is this all that I have left of him?" she had asked in anguish. "Nothing but memories of so short a time?"

And then, that last night as she had lain restless in bed, the truth had seemed to come to her with an urgency that could not be denied. For what purpose had she been born, she had asked, but to stand at his side?

All that long morning and afternoon she drove through the sullen, dun-colored countryside, till the few houses began to huddle into villages and the villages to crowd together into the wretched, poverty-stricken suburbs of the metropolis. As the cart breasted a low hill, London suddenly lay stretched below her, its hundred spires and belfries, its palaces and halls bathed in warm evening light. She could see the great river—her own river—and its bridges; she could see the gaunt pile of St. Paul's.

"It looks beautiful," she murmured in surprise. "It does not look like the city of death."

Yet, even as she murmured, the smell of death came to her from the stinking ditches on either side of the way. The shacks in this outlying district stood foul and neglected beside a midden. Few people were abroad, and those that were walked hurriedly and alone. The plague was here in this suburb. She was sure it was. She saw its fear in men's looks. She saw it in the shuttered, eyeless houses and the terrible neglect in the streets. And then she passed a watchman posted before a door. And then another. And another. And behind each watchman on the shut-up doors was painted a huge scarlet cross and the tragic prayer of the time: LORD HAVE MERCY UPON US.

Her eyes smarted; a lump rose in her throat. The horror of the plague appalled her. She was afraid. There was no disguising from herself how afraid she felt. The spires and pointed roofs of London were still a long way off. She had had no recollection from her infant memories that the capital was so vast. London seemed to her that evening to be bigger than any city had a right to be. She had miles and miles of terrible streets to drive through before she found Thomas in John Smee's house in Crooked Lane. She gritted her teeth and drove on.

The long summer evening still held the sky as she and the weary nag passed a great park where soldiers were encamped in tents. Then they entered the Tyburn Road, crossed over the Tyburn Brook, and entered the desolate parish of St. Giles-in-the-Fields, where the plague had first broken out. Here, indeed, was the valley of the shadow of death. Every other house seemed to bear its scarlet cross. In Holborn, she saw two men approaching her, carrying a coffin, and she reined in the horse to let them pass. There were so few people in the streets that she felt constrained to ask the coffin bearers where she could find Crooked Lane, but at that moment she raised her eyes and saw a gate in the city wall straight ahead of her. Crooked Lane was in the parish of St. Michael's, near Eastcheap. Thomas had told her so. And Eastcheap was within the city walls, she felt sure.

"What gate is this?" she called out to a wretched-looking boy who was hobbling towards the entrance of a dark alley.

"Newgate," he shouted back over his shoulder.

To her right rose the grim fortress of Newgate Prison. She shuddered as she surveyed its black walls. So this was where Thomas had spent so many long months when they were betrothed! Unconsciously, she had reined in the horse, which was now ambling through the gateway. In the stillness, she heard the faint sound of someone stealthily pulling something out of the back of the cart. She looked round swiftly and stared straight into the eyes of the maimed and hideous boy. He must have turned and followed her, seeing the provender she was carrying into the city, for he was now standing close behind the cart, savagely clutching a Maplehampden cheese to his chest.

"It is not for thee," she cried out in anger. "It is for the Friends."

The boy bared his teeth. He looked fiercely desperate, like a rat when it turns at bay on the dogs.

"It is for me," he screeched. "It is for me."

And he lurched away on his crippled leg, tearing at the cheese with his teeth.

Richenda, aghast at man's misery, whipped up the nag and rattled through Newgate Market and into Cheapside with the tears streaming down her cheeks. It was Thomas and the Friends she had thought to feed. But it was the whole wide world that was most sorely in need. She was terrified by the blank-faced houses on either side of her, by the closed shops, by the stillness. And then, the raving cry of a plague victim, shut up behind his scarlet cross, came to her over the noise of the cart. And the intolerable ache in her throat broke out in a sob. She had never dreamed of such a desolate hell. The few people she passed seemed hardly human; they walked in corkscrew fashion to avoid each other's contagion. They looked like ghosts, not like men.

Over all hung the smell of death.

Trembling at her danger, being a woman and alone in such a

place, she stopped by the corner of Sopar Lane and asked a watchman the way she should go.

He eyed her wildly at first—as though she and her horse and her cart of fresh vegetables were phantoms from another world.

"What are you doing here alone?" he whispered from between tight lips.

"I seek my husband in Crooked Lane."

Then he saw how it was with her and the coming child.

"Stay not a moment, mistress," he cried hoarsely, directing her into Watling Street. "At the street turn left. Carry over Walbrook into Eastcheap. Crooked Lane is on your left."

She gave him a fresh cabbage for his pains.

"Hurry, mistress," he urged her. "Dusk is falling and your horse is worth a fortune. There is not a horse left within the city walls."

❊

"Richenda!" cried Bridget Smee, running into the house yard. "Richenda, it cannot be thee!"

She was so astonished to see Richenda and the horse and cart in the dusk in the yard that she could not believe her eyes.

"Why hast thou come?" she gasped in horror. "Why has thou come, child?"

"Thomas?" whispered Richenda. "Is Thomas safe?"

"Thy Thomas?" exclaimed Bridget almost roughly. "Yes. Thy Thomas is safe!"

Then, seeing how near her unexpected guest was to her time, she suddenly gave a little cry. She held up her arms to help Richenda down and then, the tears starting up in her eyes, she hurried her indoors.

"Ephraim," she shouted to a boy in the yard. "See to the horse. Then carry all in the cart into the house."

She brought Richenda into a kitchen which was heavy with wood smoke and with some stronger vapor which Richenda could not name, and sat her down on a stool.

"Thou stopp'st nowhere in town as thou cam'st through?" she asked anxiously as she went to fetch her a mug of ale, for Richenda was coughing with the smoke.

She shook her head.

"Thomas?" she asked hoarsely, her eyes smarting with the sharp vapor. "Where is he?"

"He went forth this morning to Wood Street."

"To Wood Street," Richenda repeated blankly in a kind of trance.

"To his friend, Richard Holder, that is apprenticed to a physician there."

Richard.

So Richard was still alive! Thomas was with him! She and Thomas had prayed for Richard earnestly—passionately—in the past three months, beseeching God to spare him the contagion, for London's whole agony had been personified for them in Richard and in the London Friends. She had thought of him again and again as she had wandered alone round the Maplehampden estate, mourning Thomas's departure and the terrible danger to them both. But, during her drive through the London streets, everything had gone out of her head save the horrors she was witnessing and the image of Thomas waiting for her, strong and loving, in Crooked Lane.

But where was he now? It was evening!

"Should not Thomas be back?" she cried frantically, seeing the night deepening in the yard outside.

Bridget knelt down heavily by her side and took her clenched hands in her own.

"Thy Thomas will come presently. Thou must be calm."

Her homely, middle-aged face was puckered up with concern. Then her expression grew grave.

"Richenda, my child," she asked reprovingly. "Was it the Lord's will that thou cam'st here?"

Richenda turned away her head and gazed down at the brick floor in conscience-stricken silence. She did not know whether her intense longing for Thomas had come from the Lord— whether He had *truly* commanded her to journey to London to stand by his side. She did not know! It was a question she had dreaded all day long.

Bridget bowed her head and sighed a heavy sigh.

"My dear, my dear," she said sadly. "Thou shouldst not have come. Thy Thomas left his heart's joy safe with thee—at home, in the country."

Richenda turned again to her hostess in utter wretchedness.

"He will be angry that I have come," she wept hopelessly.

Bridget said she did not know. Yet, surely, it was madness— if it came not from the Lord. Yes, madness!—for her to have brought the child within her to London at such a time.

"Am I mad?" asked Richenda, struck by so strange a thought. "Bridget, dost thou think I am mad?"

Before she could answer, they heard footsteps in the yard and Ephraim's voice answering a spoken command. A torch flared in the darkness.

"It is Thomas!" exclaimed Richenda, rising quickly to her feet. "I am sure it is Thomas!"

Bridget, still on her knees, clutched at her skirts.

"Thou must not go to him, Richenda. Not now. Not till he

has been through the sulfur and changed his coat and washed."

Richenda tried to struggle free. She had seen Thomas's face lit up for a second by the torch. He had looked radiant, golden, shining—infinitely at peace.

"No!" cried Bridget urgently, holding firm to Richenda's dress. "Thou must do what I say—for *all* our sakes!"

It was a rule of the house, she explained hurriedly, that Thomas and her husband should fumigate themselves and change their clothes and wash before they entered. Ephraim had the things ready for them in the yard.

Richenda, listening, returned quietly to her stool.

"Forgive me, Bridget," she said uncertainly through her tears. "Please . . . forgive me. My coming . . . is . . . is a great burden to thee. A burden to you all."

And she covered her face with her hands and prayed in the darkness that Thomas would forgive her and that no harm should come to their child. She tried to lose herself in stillness, to divest herself of the earthly passions that had brought her to London, and to wait in humbleness upon the Lord.

As she sat there on the stool in the darkness, she was swept with anguish, for into the stillness of that waiting—slowly but inexorably—crept the certainty that she had deceived herself: that she had done a great wrong.

When she uncovered her face again, it was not Thomas but John Smee who stood before her, his face grim and stern.

"Richenda," he said harshly, "thou has done an ill deed to bring thyself and thy babe into this city!"

Richenda covered her face again with her hands and wept and wept. She had been a coward. She knew that she had been a coward. She had not had the courage to face life without Thomas.

"Thou has turned away from the Lord," thundered her host. "Thou has obeyed the selfish dictates of thine own heart."

His just reproof bowed her down. She had endangered the life of their child by her selfish desires. She was not worthy of Thomas. Not worthy to be a mother.

And then, in the midst of her bitter self-blame, she heard a light step beside her and a growing stillness in the room.

"Thomas," she cried.

He was leaning over her, his face tortured with grief.

"Richenda," he whispered. "Why has thou come?"

Richenda flung herself into his arms.

"Thomas," she wept. "Thomas."

Her longing for him was beyond all words to express. No words came to her save his name.

Later that night, as they lay together in Bridget Smee's guest chamber, Thomas took her in his arms.

All about them in the city crept the terrible disease. All about them in the lanes and courts men and women and children were dying a horrible death.

"Richenda, dear heart," he whispered in her ear, "I could not have wished thee here in this desolate place. But now thou are come, I am glad. Thou bringst me joy."

They were both so near death, Richenda sensed, that their lives had passed beyond the confines of reproach.

For a week longer they clung to their perilous joy, thanking God each night-time that the day had passed for them in health and that they had come to each other again. Thomas put behind him the terrible sights and sounds in the pest-house and the prisons. He kept from her the soaring figures of the deaths in the bills of mortality. And Richenda, unfitted by nature for the daily anguish of waiting for his return, stifled her agony and gave him of her best.

And then, one night, Thomas did not come back.

Richenda, dry-eyed and appalled, stared out into the darkening yard.

"He is late," said Bridget gently. "But he will yet come."

"He has been kept at Newgate," suggested John. "That is how it is."

They sat with her through the night, praying to the Lord.

That same night Richard lay on the gentle shores of sleep—not yet unconscious, but unburdened of his grief—when he was abruptly jerked back to the horrors of the times.

Someone was groaning in the street below. He listened intently, wondering whether he had heard aright. The groan came again.

He jumped out of bed and ran to his window, opened the casement, and stared down into the darkness of Wood Street. A shadow blacker than the night was huddled against the doctor's door.

"What is it, man? he shouted down. "Are you ill?"

His voice echoed over the silent roof-tops. The shadow stayed where it was, crouched on the step, making no sound.

"I will be down with you presently," he shouted at it.

Then he grabbed at his clothes. One more victim of the plague, he thought as he threw on his coat. One more poor wretch struck down in the open streets. He ran down the stairs and unlocked the doctor's front door, and, as he did so, the man fell inwards at his feet.

"Richard," sighed a familiar voice.

It was Thomas! He knelt down quickly by his side.

"Thomas!" he whispered in horror. "What ails you?"

What folly! He knew in an instant what ailed him.

"Take me . . . to . . . to the pest-house," Thomas begged, sighing again. "Richard, I beg thee, take me away."

With his deft doctor's fingers, he felt quickly over Thomas's body for the fatal swelling.

"No," he whispered hoarsely, his heart torn with grief. "You must stay here."

He lifted Thomas up and leaned him more comfortably against the jamb.

"You are too ill to move."

Thomas's whole body, propped up against the door-post, shuddered and quaked with the terrible pain of his illness.

"Not here," he croaked. "They will shut thee up if thou take me within."

And he tried to lurch away from the threshold. Richard caught him in his arms.

"I lost my way," Thomas was mumbling. "And now . . . now . . . I cannot . . . see."

He gripped Richard's hand in his own, while Richard knelt

198 · THE LORD HAVE MERCY UPON US

there at his side, sick of soul, noting the mortal pallor of Thomas's face.

"Take me to the pest-house," he muttered. "Keep me from Richenda . . ."

Richard rose gently to his feet, still holding Thomas from falling over. Then, he stooped down and gathered him up in his arms. He knew, at last, what he must do.

The doctor's horse had been stolen weeks ago. The stable was swept and empty.

"I thank thee, Richard," Thomas smiled blindly, as he carried him across the little court. "I thank thee that thou tak'st me away."

He lowered him gently onto the bare floor, took off his coat and rolled it into a bundle and put it under his head. Then, he whispered:

"I will be back in the instant. I go to the loft to fetch hay."

Thomas made no reply. He had fallen into some sort of faint. But when Richard returned with a truss of the season's hay and made a rough bed and laid Thomas on it, he opened his eyes.

"Benfield," he murmured. "The thirty-acre field."

Thomas was smiling. Richard looked at him, his heart aching with an intolerable ache, for the smell of the hay had taken him back to Benfield, too—to Richenda and Thomas and himself as children, rolling among the drying swathes of grass in the thirty-acre field.

"Where are you, Richard?" barked Dr. Boteler. "What is it that you do?"

The old man was hobbling across the courtyard with a lantern in his hand. Its beams played over the stable walls.

"I am here, sir," Richard replied. "Here, in the stable."

His master stood in the doorway in his nightcap and shift, looking down upon them both.

"The plague?" he barked.

Richard nodded his head.

The old man came over to them and knelt at Thomas's side.

"It is your young Quaker friend!" he muttered in distress.

The light seemed to trouble Thomas, for he turned away his

failing eyes. The doctor took his pulse, put his hand on his fore-head, and looked gravely at the lurid tokens on his chest.

"He has his swelling in his elbow," Richard whispered.

It had not broken. The poison had gone inwards, he ex-plained.

"I thank thee," Thomas sighed. "I thank thee, Richard, with all my heart."

"Why does he thank you?" Dr. Boteler asked.

Richard put his finger to his lips.

"He thinks I have taken him to the pest-house," he whis-pered.

The old man shook his head. Thomas was dying. Both of them knew he was dying.

"I will go and fetch him opium," the doctor said.

Thomas, too, knew that he was dying.

"Richard," he cried out suddenly, frantically groping for him with his hand. "Richard . . . thou must not leave Richenda. Richard . . . do not leave her."

Her time was almost come, he gabbled. She was alone—far from her mother.

"I will go to Richenda," Richard assured him, grasping his burning hand. "I will see that no harm come to her . . . ever."

Thomas grew a little calmer. His head rolled back among the wisps of hay.

"Thou must love her, too," he whispered.

He was now rolling his head from side to side—as Richard had seen so many other victims of the plague do in the last two months. Thomas was nearing his end.

"Thou always loved'st Richenda," he said, smiling.

Richard bent over him and wiped the sweat off his forehead.

"Richenda, dearest Richenda," Thomas murmured faintly. "Thou has great need . . . of love."

By the time that Dr. Boteler returned to the stable, there was no need for his opium.

Thomas was dead.

In the gray dawn, Richenda, stark-eyed with watching, stared out into the yard unaware that the shadows were fading and that the wall of the court was growing pale with the coming day. On either side of her, Bridget and John Smee sat fast asleep, worn out by their patient vigil.

"He will not come now," she told herself. "He is dead. Thomas is dead. I shall not see him again."

A terrible calm gripped her heart. It was as though her blood were frozen—as though Thomas's not coming to her had drained her of emotion.

"Thomas is dead," she repeated over and over again, understanding the words, knowing what they meant—but not *feeling* them on her pulse; not feeling them anywhere.

While she sat there in her stony despair she heard the outer gate of the courtyard creak, and presently a young man strode towards the house door. She stared at him, incurious. He was tall and strong and yet bent with fatigue. Deep furrows of care were grooved in his sallow cheeks.

"Bridget," she heard herself say, "there is a stranger come to the door."

Bridget woke in a daze, looked in panic at the paling sky, and then, with a sob, gazed at Richenda. Then she looked out of the window at the young man.

"I know him not," she said.

She went to the door. Dully, Richenda heard the man's voice. Unmoved, she heard Bridget drawing in her breath quickly in horror.

"Thomas is dead," she said to herself again. "The stranger has come to tell us so."

John was awake by now. He had joined his wife.

Bridget came back to her in the kitchen and stood in front of her, speaking words. But Richenda seemed suddenly deaf. She could hear nothing Bridget said. She could only read the dreadful tidings in her eyes, in her tears, in the anguished twist of her mouth.

"Richenda," she heard at last, "thou must go speak to him. Speak to him through the window. He will not come in."

Richenda rose slowly. John opened the window. And she stood in the growing light, feeling the cool air of the new day brushing against her cheek. She looked, uncomprehendingly, into the eyes of the stranger.

"Richenda," said Richard brokenly, "I have brought . . . terrible news."

She did not start or cry out.

"Richard," she sighed, "it is thee."

He was changed past all knowing.

"Thomas died an hour ago," he said, turning away his face. He could not bear to see her stricken grief.

"I know," she whispered. "I knew he was dead."

"In the stable. In my arms."

She stood staring at him, her heart still frozen by despair. She saw the anguish in the turn of his head. And suddenly, his sorrow touched her.

"It was a heavy grief," she said slowly. "A heavy grief for thee to tell me, Richard."

He looked at her, at once, straight in the face. A single tear was slowly trickling down her cheek. Bridget, standing behind her, had taken her in her arms.

"I will come to you again, Richenda," said Richard. "I will not leave you."

14
❈ New Life

In the days following Thomas's death Richenda
lived in a wasteland. She got up in the morning, dressed, picked
at the food that was offered her, and moved from room to
room in the Smees' dark London house, trying to carry out the
few easy domestic duties which Bridget—out of pity—had set
aside for her. But day after day she fell into desolate dreams
and awoke to find herself sitting in a chair, staring at nothing
—knowing that she had sat there for hours, lost in her anguished longing for Thomas. "Thou must teach thyself to
work, child," said her host to her one day. His voice was stern
but not unkind. "In work, the Lord has given us a cure to help
us through our grief." But Richenda, try as she might, could
not find an opiate in Bridget's housework. Her grief was too
new. The suddenness and completeness of Thomas's departure
appalled her. He had kissed her in the morning while she was
yet in bed, giving her his grave and loving salute. And then he
had gone. Gone forever! There was nothing left of him. Nothing at all—save his shoes for the house, his second shirt, a pair
of stockings, and his Bible. She could not bear to look at these
pitiful leavings. She could not endure the dwindling of her

treasure, in so rare and radiant a man, to these few plain objects he had used.

"Richenda, dear heart," Bridget reminded her gently, "thou hast his child."

The child moved strongly within her. She felt it kicking at night. She knew that she wanted the child; that she would give it love; that she would devote her whole future life to this being whom they had both created.

But this being within her was not Thomas.

It was Thomas she wanted.

From the top of the bleakest peak of despair she had ever scaled, she looked down upon the empty years unrolling below her. She saw the vast desert of her future life and the stony journey she must make without Thomas at her side.

How long—how endlessly long—stretched a human life!

"Isaac is seventy-six," she whispered, terrified at the thought. "And I am twenty-one!"

She might have fifty-five years before she could come to Thomas again.

All about her London was enduring its agony. The bells no longer tolled for the dead, for they would have tolled all day and all night had each man's passing been thus mourned. Deaths from the plague at the end of August had risen to a terrible seven thousand five hundred a week. The graveyards were full. The dead-carts no longer toured the streets only by night, but carried the corpses, uncoffined, to the plague pits in the broad light of day. Death was no longer remarkable. It was life and health that were strangers.

"Richenda, let me tell you how it was," said Richard, standing outside in the courtyard and speaking to her through the open window. "Let me tell you how it was with Thomas since he came to London."

And Richenda, vaguely grateful that he should have come and yet strangely numb and unresponsive to anything anyone said to her, nodded her head and bade him tell her.

She must have understood Thomas's courage, he said. But what she could not know was his extraordinary quickness in learning to tend the sick. Dr. Boteler had only had to explain a treatment for Thomas at once to grasp the reason why it was prescribed. And he was so deft with his clumsy scholar's fingers and so compassionate and calm—even with those in delirium— that he had brought comfort and peace to the wretched wherever he had gone.

"I do not understand how he could have endured what he did," said Richard in sad wonder. "He was always so hurt by others' pain."

And then, on that last night, he continued, when Thomas knew that he was stricken with the plague, it was not of himself that he had thought, but of her and of Dr. Boteler and of Richard himself. He had been trying to find his way to the city pest-house near St. Luke's, he had told him.

"But he must have been so dazed by his illness," Richard said, "that he had lost his sense of direction, for he was far out of his way there."

"And he came to thee?"

"Stumbled there, more likely—by chance."

They stood, the two of them, on either side of Bridget Smee's kitchen window and thought unhappily of the Thomas whom they had both loved, in those last, terrible hours of his life, staggering ill and lost in a city made desolate by the plague.

"He would not let me carry him within," continued Richard, "for fear of the danger to us both."

Richenda nodded her head, wordlessly. What he said seemed to her a twice-told tale. It was as though she had heard it all before.

"So I picked him up . . . and carried him . . . carried him to the stable."

She saw Richard staggering across the night-dark court with Thomas in his arms. It was not so heavy a burden, she thought. Thomas was light. Besides, he had done it before. At Benfield. When they were twelve. When Thomas fell off the barn roof and twisted his knee.

"He died so quietly!" Richard was saying. "So much at peace! He smiled . . . thinking only of you."

Richenda bowed her head. If the tears could have flowed, they would have tumbled down like the waters of the Maple-hampden weir at his words. But she could not cry. Her grief had scorched her tears.

When she looked back at that time in London after Thomas's death, she realized that Richard must have come almost every day to talk with her through the open window—yet, at the time, she was so dazed by her loss that an hour after he had left she had forgotten that he had been there. She remembered only that someone had made her think of Benfield and that for a brief instant in all that arid waste of days and nights she had revisited the green places of their childhood and played again with Thomas by the Thames.

September came. And, with the new month, the number of deaths from the plague in London soared to eight thousand a week. Richenda, living at the very heart of this woe in the dark Quaker house in Crooked Lane, wondered whether God had forsaken the world she knew.

Early in the morning of September 3, as she lay staring without hope at the dawn creeping across the walls of her chamber, she felt herself clutched by a cramp. It made her gasp with surprise. She had never imagined a pain quite like it. Then she thought:

It is the plague. I have the plague.

A terrible cramp often heralded the plague. John Smee had told her so.

The pain ebbed slowly away. But when a second attack gripped her she gave herself up to it joyfully, suddenly aware that God had not forsaken her. He had given her the plague, she thought. If God were kind, she would die. She would be with Thomas in a matter of hours. She felt like something thrown into a wild sea. She was borne swiftly up to a crest of pain and then suddenly dropped into a trough of nothingness where—beyond belief—she thought she must have slept, till the next surge of cramp bore her up to the crest again.

What a strange way to journey to Thomas, she thought dizzily.

And then, with a jab of pain far sharper than the rest—so

that she nearly cried out—she suddenly realized that it was not the plague. It was the child. Thomas's child.

She lay back trembling with surprise, and then, hearing in the still dawn the sound of Bridget raking out the kitchen fire, she struggled to the door and cried out:

"Bridget. Bridget."

Exhausted by the effort of shouting, she stumbled back to bed and, in a sudden, blessed cessation of pain, felt herself plummeting down into the trough of nothingness. She awoke minutes later to a new gale of anguish and to people moving hurriedly about the room. Bridget was stooping over her.

"Oh, Thomas!" wept Richenda. "I wish Thomas were here."

Someone had put a cool hand on her forehead.

"His child will soon be with thee," said Bridget gently.

His child! Thomas's child! Richenda took the news with her into the vortex of the storm. Five minutes later, buffeted almost beyond bearing and reeling from the waves, she felt herself thrown up and abandoned on a far shore.

Through the stillness came the howling of a child.

"Richenda, thou hast a son!" exclaimed Bridget joyfully.

"A son!" gasped Richenda, sitting straight up in bed. "Is he all right? Is he safe? Give him to me quickly."

Bridget had her back to her; she was wrapping her howling son in a shawl.

"Tcht! Tcht!" she said, smiling as she turned round and handed her the bundle. "Here he is, complete with ten fingers and ten toes and a wisp of his father's dark hair."

Richenda gazed enraptured at a pink and wrinkled little creature whose face was contorted with rage. But even as she held him, marvelling that she and Thomas should have created such a perfect being, the baby's face uncreased, he opened his screwed-up eyes, looked at his mother—and yawned.

"He's yawning!" exclaimed Richenda incredulously. "Bridget, my son's yawning!"

The two days following Tom's birth were days of strange animal bliss. Richenda slept as she had not slept for weeks and months. It was as though, in an instant, she fell soundlessly to the bottom of a deep well of sleep, from which Bridget hauled her up every four hours to attend to the child.

"He is hungry; he must be fed," she said, laughing gently. "Thy son is a very glutton for living."

And Richenda, who had wakened every morning before his birth to a new agony at Thomas's death, now wakened to discover afresh the miracle of his son. The child had Thomas's dark eyes—and his nose—and his chin. She discovered that his fingernails were like tiny, perfect, sea-washed shells and that his brains seemed to be pulsing through his skull.

"All babies' heads are so," Bridget reassured her quickly, seeing her panic-stricken gaze.

Yet even more of a revelation to her than his tiny, exquisite body were her own emotions towards her son. This child was her own. She had given him life. Only through the milk in her breasts could he continue to live. No one on earth had ever been so dependent upon her before. Every four hours she took the baby from Bridget's arms and gave him suck with a fierce tenderness that she had never felt before—not even for Thomas. She was overwhelmed by her love for him. Yet out of this love and out of his utter helplessness crept a fear that she had thought she had banished forever from her life. For when Thomas had died she had thought: The worst in life has now happened. Thomas is dead. I can fear for him no longer. Her loss had brought her the calm of despair. She had known that she could face her parents' death with courage and that her own meant nothing to her at all—save a release: God's loving answer to her prayer that she should join Thomas soon.

But now the child in her arms had cast out despair. She, Richenda, must live. She must live to protect the child from the terrible world about them. As she gazed down upon him while he sucked at her breast, Tom's ignorance—his utter unawareness of the misery into which he had been born—made a great lump swell in her throat. He yawned and sneezed at plague-stricken London. Fatherless forever, he looked up into her face and smiled. His innocence appalled her. It made her clutch him frenziedly in an agony of fear for him.

Two days after his birth Richenda awoke in the late evening

from her deep, childbed sleep to find no one in her chamber save the child, asleep in Bridget's old family cradle close by her side. He looked comfortable and well. Yet Richenda's waking instinct was one of anguished terror.

Something was wrong. Terribly wrong.

She lay listening to the quiet sounds coming from the kitchen below and looked again at the peaceful child and wondered why she felt so frightened.

And then, she looked upward at the bedroom ceiling—and she knew!

Across the ceiling swept billows of red, dancing light, reflected up from the city outside. The air, she realized suddenly, was heavy with the smell of wood smoke and burning tar.

She jumped out of bed and snatched up the sleeping child. Through the window streamed the glare of a dozen fires. She ran in panic to the head of the stairs.

"Bridget! Bridget!" she shouted. "The whole lane is alight!"

She heard a clatter of pans below and the kitchen door pulled roughly open. Then someone was springing up the curve of the stairs in stockinged feet.

It was Richard.

"Richenda," he shouted. "Don't panic! Don't panic!"

She looked infinitely fragile and young and defenseless to him, standing there terrified at the top of the stairs with the child in her arms.

"They have lit fires in the streets on purpose," he told her as he took her shoulders gently and guided her back to her chamber. "Do not fret. It is to smoke out the plague."

Richenda found herself shaking all over and the tears rolling down her cheeks.

"Let me take the baby," he said quietly. "You are upset. I will lay him back in his cradle."

She crept back under the sheet, her teeth chattering still with her fright—and with anger seizing her heart. For some reason which she could not understand, she could not bear Richard to see her terror: to guess how vulnerable she was because of the child; what a coward she had become because of Tom.

"It is the Lord Mayor's proclamation," he was saying as he

bent over Tom's cradle to tuck him in. "Every group of twelve households in the city is responsible for lighting and tending a fire. They are to burn without stop for three whole days."

He lingered at his task, gazing at Thomas's and Richenda's baby with aching affection. He was such a rumpled-looking little thing.

"Will it do any good?" Richenda asked absently, while she tried to understand her rage.

What did it matter what Richard thought of her? she wondered.

"No good at all," he laughed bitterly.

"Why do they do it?"

He shrugged his shoulders.

"It is the latest cure for the plague come out of France," he replied. "*Smoke* out the plague—that's what they say."

It would do no good, he continued, for the plague was not in the air, as so many people thought. It was carried by the fleas on men's bodies and harbored in their clothes. It was in the sewers and cellars and middens and behind the wainscot—wherever the rats that carried the fleas had their haunts.

He turned back to her from the cradle and caught her staring in open-eyed horror at the wainscot round the room.

"Richenda," he said sternly, "this is a clean, sound house. You know it is. The Smees stopped up their rat-holes months ago."

She smiled at him uncertainly, ashamed of her terror—and yet, at the same time, oddly comforted that he should reprove her.

Slowly, this man who had once been their childhood friend was swimming into focus in her mind.

The fires in the streets burned night and day from September 5 until the afternoon of the 8th, when they were quenched—as though at heaven's command—by a deluge of rain so heavy and prolonged that it filled the narrow lanes with billows of steam and smoke and flooded the gutters and swirled away the filth. In the middle of the month the weekly deaths still stood at over eight thousand. God's anger with his Englishmen seemed never-ending. Yet His mercy was at hand, for with the colder weather of October the dreadful onslaught of the plague was spent. Deaths fell sharply to a thousand a week. London crept back into the daylight.

Early in November, John Smee set out for Benfield in the farm cart with Richenda and Tom. As they drove through the long-deserted streets, they saw that grass was beginning to grow up between the cobble-stones.

Richenda held the child tight in her arms. She hoped that neither of them would ever set eyes on London again.

"My dearest child, my dearest child," murmured Isaac as Richenda bent over his chair to kiss his forehead.

He was crippled with rheumatism and nearly blind. With his hand, he felt over her hair and cheek and chin.

"Thou art thin, Richenda. Thou must rest and eat."

"She is well enough," said Susannah calmly. "She will grow strong now that she has come to us."

She spoke a little absently, as though Richenda's health could very well be left to take care of itself. She had her grandson in her arms. It was upon Tom that she was pouring out her love.

Richenda, turning from her stepfather to look at her mother, was melted almost to tears by her mother's solemn joy.

She loves him, she thought rapturously. She loves him—almost as much as I do.

And, on the instant, she knew that she loved her mother for loving her son more deeply than she had ever loved her before.

Yet this quiet homecoming was encompassed about with sorrow. Thomas was dead. He had left them forever. Each one of them spoke and moved and acted with the bitter consciousness of their loss. For Richenda, coming back to Benfield brought her face to face with the true nature of her bereavement. Here, in surroundings which they had loved and shared, everything spoke to her of Thomas. She had only to sit down for a moment at her stepfather's study table for her to see at once a childish Thomas grinning at her over the top of his Latin primer. She had only to step out into the dreary autumn garden to be back in an August morning fifteen months ago, sitting by his

side on the wooden seat and sniffing the scent of the newly cut
box hedge. She wandered by the river. *This* was where he and
Richard had fished. It was his favorite part. She slipped
through the farm gate to the meeting house and stared at the
brick wall they had built together. She rode moodily along the
valley towards Maplehampden—and remembered their wedding day. Sorrow was an ache everlasting.

"Oh, Richenda, dear heart," Isaac whispered as she helped
him up the stairs to bed, "I am old and I long for death. Yet
the Lord will not take me."

What grieved their hearts they left unsaid.

The Lord had taken Thomas—at twenty-one—in the pride
and vigor of his young life.

Within a month Richenda was back at Maplehampden. It was
right and proper, she said, that Tom should grow up in his father's house. Besides, the estate needed a master.

"But, Richenda," protested her mother, "what know'st *thou*
of running an estate? Thou art a woman. And alone."

"I shall learn what I have to learn," she replied sharply.
"Thou hast managed Benfield all these years. Why should I not
manage Maplehampden?"

"It is four times the size."

"Then I must work four times the harder."

Stout words. But, as she said them, she knew that it was impossible to work four times as hard as her mother had worked
when she, Richenda, was a girl.

"I will seek thy help . . . often," she smiled more humbly.
"Very often."

Though she could scarcely bear to have Tom out of her
sight, she steeled herself to leave him with Frances, the young
nursemaid, every morning and again in the afternoon, while she
rode abroad to inspect her fields and direct the management of
her farms. Her folk helped her. They taught her what they
could. Gone were the sullen looks that had greeted them both
when they had first come to the house. First respect, then trust,
and, last, grief at their young master's death had earned her a
place in their affections. They would give her a trial, she

thought, if only for the sake of their young master's son. There was an Egerton back in the nursery. They would work honestly and well for the child.

Yet it was a lonely time and one fraught often with sudden panic, for when she was far from home, visiting some distant farm, a teror would suddenly possess her soul.

What if the house be alight! her mind would shriek. What if the flames are licking up the staircase! What if Frances cannot carry him through the fire!

And she would turn her horse, spurring it most cruelly, and gallop back through the gray winter light, her heart pounding wildly and her eyes piercing the gloom for the first glimpse of the Maplehampden chimneys. When she saw that there was no smoke in the air beneath the clouds and that the roof and the windows were whole, she would not stay her course, but go clattering down the village street, past the smithy and through the church gate, throw down her reins by the great oak door, and run panting up the stairs.

"Frances, Frances, how's Tom? Is he safe?"

"The child is well, mistress," the girl would answer, smiling her slow smile. "Even now he has been smiling at his toes."

Or:

"He sleeps, mistress. He has slept ever since you left."

And the two of them would stand by the heavy oak cradle in which so many of the child's forebears had been rocked, and gaze down in thankfulness at Thomas's son.

15
❖ The Weir Bridge

RICHENDA dreaded Richard's first visit to Benfield.
She knew that he was coming, for Isaac and Susannah, choosing
a sunny day in that stormy May, had driven down the valley in
the ancient coach to acquaint her of the fact.

"Dr. Boteler has given him leave to come to us for a space,"
her mother had said.

Richenda had frowned.

"Art thou not pleased, child?" her mother had asked
sharply. "He was once thy friend."

She had answered that she was indeed pleased. And so she
was. But she was frightened, too. She was frightened that Richard would expect too much of her: that he would ask her to
give what she no longer had it in her power to give to any man.
She had found a kind of calm—a meager peace in her anxious
care of Thomas's estate. And she did not wish to be disturbed.

Besides, Tom was the sun of her life. He was her sun by day
and her moon by night. She did not really want another planet
in her universe.

Two days later she stood at the nursery window and saw that
Richard had already come. He had ridden down the valley. He
was standing in the courtyard, immediately below her, tying his

reins to the iron staple in the wall. She picked up the child and walked slowly down the stairs to meet him. Tom was making high, chattering noises, like a goldfinch, as they went. And he had grasped a handful of her cheek in his fist.

"Richenda!" exclaimed Richard in delight. "And Tom!"

She looked so beautiful to him, standing there with the child grabbing at her face and her hair escaping untidily from her velvet cap, that he wanted to throw his arms round her. She was superb. Both defenseless and strong. Quite unaware of her own power.

Thank God I can at least kiss the child, he thought, taking Tom from her arms and cradling him in his own.

Tom was like his father, he said. Just look at those deep, wide eyes! And his brow! And the slight cleft in his chin!

"You're an Egerton, all right!" he laughed.

And Tom, staring up in wonder at the strange face, suddenly opened his mouth and laughed back.

Richenda, delighted at Richard's pleasure in her child, prayed silently to God to keep him so.

Dear God, she said. Don't make him impatient and pushing —as he always was. Please keep him just quietly loving Tom.

Heaven lent him wisdom. He carried the child into the great hall and introduced him to the portraits of his ancestors.

"That's Sir Crispin, Tom," he said. "He smelled out money with that great nose of his. You'll come to thank him for it when you're older."

Richenda watched them, strangely at peace. The child was happy in his arms. He was stretching out his hand towards the pictures and crooning his bird-talk at them.

"And that's Sir Orlando, who built you your beautiful house," Richard continued. "And that's Sir Vivian, who got you your baronetcy. What do you think of him, Sir Tom?"

"No, cried Richenda indignantly. "He's *not* Sir Tom. Thou forget'st he is born a Friend. Friends scorn the vanity of titles."

The old Richenda! thought Richard as he bowed solemnly to the child in his arms.

"I crave thy pardon, Friend Tom," he smiled. "Thy father's friend is still a fool."

And he wandered on round the room till he stood with the
boy before the portrait of Sir James—flushed with valor, his
breastplate winking at them from the painter's shadows. What
was Sir James's gift to his grandson? Richard shook his head.
He did not know. Sir James had brought nothing but grief.

Richenda watched his eyes rest sadly on the empty wall beyond.

"There's no portrait of him anywhere," she said, answering
his thought. "Not even a miniature. I've hunted everywhere."

"You'd have thought his mother would have had the likeness
of her only son."

Richenda shook her head.

"There's not even a pencil sketch of Thomas," she said sorrowfully.

They walked out into the garden together, Richard still holding the child, and stood staring nostalgically at the flashing Thames.

"Tom will have to be our portrait of him," Richard said quietly. "As he grows older he'll grow more like him still."

And they fell to talking about Thomas: of his hopes; and his courage; and his faith.

Richard wooed Richenda with an exquisite patience—born of love.

She is like a grayling, he thought when he came to her again in August. The least shadow on the water sends her darting for cover in the water weeds.

He had found Thomas's rod in the gun room and the two of them were sitting on the bank of the Thames, while Tom staggered about on his unsteady legs in the meadow behind them and collapsed laughing among the water mints.

"Hush, Tom, he's fishing," Richenda said, putting a finger to her lips.

Richard told her to let the child be. He liked laughter. It was good to hear laughter again. And as for the fish, they could all leap up in the river and laugh at him, too, for all he cared.

"How strange!" she smiled. "Thou wast always so serious with thy fishing when we were young."

The past! It was always with them! Richard saw that it was Richenda's refuge. He saw—as he had seen so often in London during the past nine months—that the plague had exacted a terrible toll: that she was still shocked, bruised, and infinitely afraid.

He talked of the present and of the future very seldom and with great tact.

"I shall be out of my apprenticeship this time next year," he told her that afternoon.

"What then wilt thou do?"

He shrugged his shoulders.

"Mend bodies that are sick," he said.

"In London?" she asked almost eagerly. "Thou wilt get fame, Richard. I know thou wilt!"

"Do you think I want fame?" he asked sadly.

"Dost thou not?" she asked in surprise.

He would much rather live at Maplehampden and tend the countryfolk. But, looking at Richenda, he held his peace.

He was gone before the month was out.

Three days later Richenda, out riding on Hampden Hill, saw that the sky had darkened and thickened to the southeast. Was it a storm? A hurricane? Her horse raised his head; then sniffed and neighed. So strange was the eastern darkness in the blaze of noon that she returned to the hill in the evening. The whole evening sky towards London was full of orange smoke. She could smell it now—the terrible acrid smell of burning tallow, oil, wood, and tar.

"The city must be on fire!" she exclaimed, aghast.

Bridget! John!—and Richard! What was happening to Richard under that terrible pall of smoke?

She rode back down the hill to Maplehampden and then galloped wildly through the dusk to Benfield.

Yes. London was on fire, her mother said. The road through the hills was crowded with people bringing their furniture away in carts. Half of London Bridge had gone! And thirty churches. Men feared for St. Paul's.

"And Crooked Lane? And Wood Street?" Richenda cried in panic.

Her mother shook her head. There was no end for any of them of the terrors of life.

"I know nothing of Crooked Lane and Wood Street, child," she said. "They seemed crazed with fear—the people on the road."

In the anguished week of waiting for news of Richard and the Smees, Richenda awoke from the lethargy of her grief. She came to realize what she should have realized straightaway after Thomas's death: that one has to learn to live with pain, with the terrible disasters and shocks which are the lot of men and women. She saw, too—in sharp remorse—that one must reach out one's hands to the people one is fond of, speak to them, treasure them, bring them happiness before death closed over their heads and it was too late. Richard was precious to her—not only for the past. If ever he came out alive from that pall of smoke, she would try to tell him so.

When she heard at last that he was safe, and the Smees safe, too, though both had lost their homes and all that they possessed, she sat down on a kitchen chair at Benfield and gave silent, heartfelt thanks to God for His mercy. And later that night, when she was safely back at Maplehampden in bed—in their bridal chamber—Thomas came to her more vividly than he had ever come to her since his death. She was right, he told her. She must not waste God's gift of life in grieving for his death. Life was for living; not for weeping.

Yet life as she had once known it—with all its vivid joy and ache—was slow in coming back to her, young and healthy though she was. She knew, that autumn, that she was smelling the bonfires once again, and when she rode through the winter woods the old familiar scent of rotting leaves and moss and fungus came to her, flung up by her horse's hoofs. In springtime she heard the thrush's song.

Yet these were not enough, for these brought merely the pain of remembered joy.

It was only Tom who brought her a present happiness: Tom smiling all over his body when she came into the room; Tom running into her arms; Tom first clumsily mouthing and then gabbling her name.

It was in Tom that she truly lived . . . and in the hope that Richard would come to her again.

It was September again now, and the three of them were down by the weir bridge. Richard and Richenda were sitting on the grass, and the child was running hither and thither over the wide lawn at their back. Before them flashed the hurrying Thames.

"It is very strange!" Richenda said.

Her face was flushed and her heart was thudding with joy—for the one grievous obstacle to their love seemed, by his words, to have suddenly been removed.

"I was a great fool when I was young," Richard replied, smiling in mockery at himself.

He had thought of religion, he continued, as something that was inextricably bound up with class and culture and political beliefs. And he had thought that men owed their duty to these before they owed it to their consciences.

"I thought being an obedient subject to the king overrode being an obedient subject to one's God."

"And now?"

She found herself trembling as she waited for him to go on.

"Thomas has taught me otherwise," he replied.

Thomas had taught him that if one had the courage to love one's God in adversity one also had the courage to love God's creatures: to love and succor them even in the valley of death.

"The plague was like the burning fiery furnace, Richenda. Only those with faith withstood the test."

Richenda looked at him, much puzzled.

"But, Richard . . . thou . . . thou and Dr. Boteler . . . you were both brave men . . ."

"And we have not your faith?"

Richenda nodded her head.

"We believe in mankind."

He smiled a little wryly.

"It is a faith in which we are much strained at times. But—there it is!"

And since he believed in mankind, he continued, he believed that each man had a right to worship God in the manner that his conscience told him.

"Dost thou mean that even Mohammedans have the right to worship God as they think fit?" she exclaimed excitedly.

"Certainly!"

"Goodness!" she said, staring at him in wonder. "That's what Thomas thought, too!"

Deeply happy at last, and marvelling at the way ideas and people and life itself came full circle, Richenda tore her eyes from Richard for a second and gazed over the sunlit river.

"Richard!" she gasped. "Richard!"

No sound came to her voice. She clutched frantically at his arm. She stared at him stark-eyed with horror.

Tom was standing far out on the terrible weir bridge. He was all alone. He was standing on the narrow plank, two feet above the falling water. He had turned his head. He was looking back at them—smiling—pleased with himself.

Richard dashed to his feet.

"Don't call out," he told her. "Don't say a word. Smile at him."

He ran to the bank and then stopped dead. He was a heavy man. He must tread with care. The plank whipped up like a lash—he remembered that.

Dear God. Dear God, prayed Richenda, as she watched Richard put one foot down gently in front of the other. Dear God, don't let Tom drown.

Richard moved out from the bank with infinite care, talking to Tom over the sound of the water.

"Stand firm on your two feet, Tom. That's the way a man stands on a bridge."

But the child could not hear. He was entranced by the water. He was bending down so that he could look at it closer. And, as he bent down, he looked upside down at Richenda and tried to tell her his joy.

Richenda stood on the bank, dizzy with terror. Two September days blurred in her mind. It was not Tom; it was Thomas who was out on the bridge—smudge-eyed, frightened, valiant Thomas. She shut her eyes for a second in utter panic. Her whole life—everyone she loved—was out on that horrible plank.

She opened them to a cruel, sunlit world. Richard had almost reached the child, but Tom, looking up and seeing him close at hand, gave him a mischievous look with his father's dark eyes, got firmly onto his legs, and skipped away towards the Berkshire bank.

"Steady, Tom, Steady. I am not so fast as you," Richard called after him cheerfully, as he continued to creep heavily and yet delicately over the flimsy bridge.

He caught up with him at last where he had caught up with Tom's father—in the bank of nettles on the farther side.

Richenda, with tears of relief and happiness streaming down her cheeks, heard Tom's screams of anger as the nettles stung him.

"Carry him back over the ford," she shouted through her cupped hands. "I'll meet thee there."

"Dearest Richenda," said Richard, as he walked up from the ford with Tom perched upon his shoulder. "I bring you our son —Thomas's, yours, and . . . mine."

She flung her arms round him.

"Oh, Richard, dear Richard, I thought thou wast never going to say that."

He kissed her firmly and long, even though Tom was tugging at his hair.

"But I have one task to do before we wed," he said at last.

"What's that?" she asked, laughing.

"I must do it this instant," he said, giving Richenda the child. "Do what?"

"Cut down that terrible bridge."

About the Author

The distinguished novelist Hester Burton is known on both sides of the Atlantic for her rare ability to recreate the past in vivid and memorable terms. She won the Carnegie Medal in England for *Time of Trial; In Spite of All Terror* was chosen as a Notable Book of 1969 by the American Library Association; and she has received many other honors and awards for her writing. An Oxford graduate herself, Mrs. Burton is married to an Oxford don, a classicist who shares her interest in history. The Burtons live in Kidlington, England.

About the Illustrator

Victor G. Ambrus lives in Hampshire, England, near Basingstoke and Reading, where much of the action in BEYOND THE WEIR BRIDGE takes place. He describes the countryside as "real civil war country, where every other village inn or church still bears bullet holes and other relics of Cromwell's troops." He has even begun a small collection, including a sword and bits of armor, from this period—a favorite period for Mr. Ambrus.

Born in Budapest, Victor Ambrus attended the Hungarian Academy of Fine Art. He left Hungary after the 1956 uprisings and continued his studies at the Royal College of Art in London. Although principally a free-lance illustrator, Mr. Ambrus also lectures at the Guildford School of Art in Surrey. He has illustrated many children's books, and in 1965 received the British Library Association's Kate Greenaway Medal for that year's most outstanding illustrated book for children.